Twayne's United States Authors Series

Sylvia E. Bowman, *Editor*

INDIANA UNIVERSITY

William Ellery Channing

WILLIAM ELLERY CHANNING

WILLIAM ELLERY CHANNING

by **ARTHUR W. BROWN**
Utica College of Syracuse University

 7

Twayne Publishers, Inc.   ::   New York

MANUFACTURED IN THE UNITED STATES OF AMERICA BY
UNITED PRINTING SERVICES, INC.
NEW HAVEN, CONN.

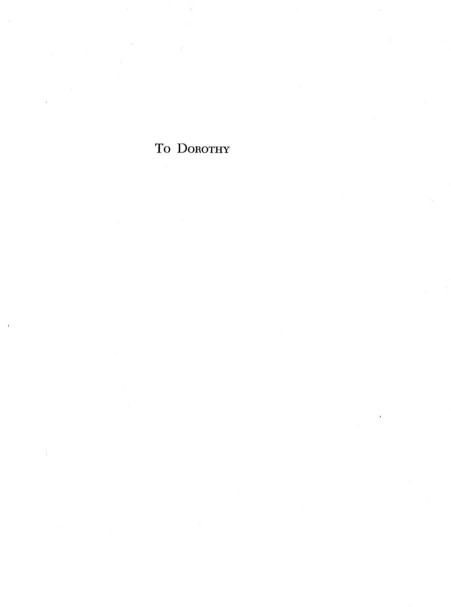

To Dorothy

Preface

THE PURPOSE of the present study is to continue the redefinition of William Ellery Channing's life and work that has been going on during the past decade. Until 1950, the name of Dr. Channing was at best but vaguely familiar to most Americans of the present age, and even scholars of American culture confused him with his namesake and nephew, William Ellery Channing, the poet-companion of Emerson and Thoreau. Since that time, a reawakening of interest in Channing has been shown by Robert L. Patterson's treatment of Channing's thought, *The Philosophy of William Ellery Channing*, by David Edgell's "intellectual portrait," and by the present writer's biography, *Always Young for Liberty*. As a result, something has been accomplished in restoring a proper balance between the enthusiastic approbation of Channing's contemporaries and the neglect into which he had fallen in the first half of the twentieth century.

Much still remains to be done before Channing occupies his proper place in the history of American thought. Very little of his published work is now available, and most of that appears in anthologies, where it is buried among that of contemporaries more renowned for their literary accomplishments than he. It is now time for his writings to become better known to a generation who will certainly appreciate the love of liberty that guided his defense of human rights. My earnest hope is that the following exposition will lead to a new edition of his basic writings by removing him from the limbo of "transition figures" and placing him where he belongs—at the center of the intellectual and cultural movements of the new nation emerging into world history in the nineteenth century.

In preparing this volume I owe thanks to many people who have helped me with suggestions and judicious criticism. To list everyone is not possible, but I should like all to know how much I appreciate their help. I shall always be indebted to Professor Edwin H. Cady, who first encouraged me to write about Channing; and I wish especially to thank my colleagues at Utica College who have made my work easier. To the personnel of the Boston Public Library, the Houghton Library and the Divinity School Library at Harvard University, the Massachusetts Historical Society and the Rhode Island Historical Society, I am under deep obligation. My special thanks for prompt and obliging service goes to Miss Mary Dudley of the Utica College Library.

To Mr. Henry M. Channing of Sherborn, Massachusetts, who now possesses the finest collection of Channing manuscripts and who is doing his part to keep his ancestor's memory alive by establishing a Channing Memorial in Boston, I wish to acknowledge my gratitude for meaningful insights into Channing's life and times as well as for his kind permission to quote from original sources.

Finally, my gratitude to the Syracuse University Press for allowing me to quote from copyrighted material in *Always Young For Liberty.*

ARTHUR WAYNE BROWN

Utica, New York
November, 1960

Contents

Chronology

1780   Born in Newport, Rhode Island, April 7.

1792   Studies with his uncle, Henry Channing, at New London, Connecticut. Father dies.

1798   Graduates from Harvard at head of class. Delivers address on "The Present Age" at commencement.

1798-   Tutor in Randolph family, Richmond, Virginia. First-
1800   hand acquaintance with slavery and Jeffersonian supporters.

1800   Returns to Newport. Studies divinity and becomes friend of Reverend Samuel Hopkins.

1802   Studies theology in Cambridge.

1803   Ordained and installed in Federal Street Church, Boston, June 1.

1812   Anti-war sermon.

1814   Married to his cousin, Ruth Gibbs, July 21, 1814. Preaches at King's Chapel on fall of Napoleon.

1815   Beginning of "Unitarian Controversy." Channing writes letters defending liberal position to Samuel Thacher and Samuel Worcester.

1819   Preaches Baltimore Sermon on "Unitarian Christianity" at ordination of Jared Sparks.

1820   Harvard awards him an honorary doctorate in divinity.

1821   Delivers Dudleian lecture at Harvard, which impresses young Waldo Emerson.

1822-   Travels for health in England and on continent. Meets
1823   Wordsworth, Coleridge, Southey, Lucy Aikin.

1824   Ezra Stiles Gannett becomes colleague.

1825   American Unitarian Association organized. Channing declines to become first president.

1826   Publishes "Remarks on the Character of John Milton."

1827- Publishes "Remarks on the Life and Character of
1828 Napoleon Bonaparte."

1828 Preaches sermon on "Likeness to God," the most transcendental of any public utterance.

1829 Publishes "Remarks on the Character and Writings of Fénelon" and an address on "The Union."

1830 Preaches Election Sermon on "Spiritual Freedom." Publishes "The Importance and Means of a National Literature" and *Discourses, Reviews, and Miscellanies.*

1830- Visits West Indies and sees slavery under English
1831 system.

1832 Publishes second volume of sermons.

1834 Mother dies on May 25.

1835 Publishes "Slavery." Marks beginning of active antislavery efforts. Publishes sermon on war.

1836 Publishes "The Abolitionists," an open letter to James B. Birney.

1837 Writes open letter to Henry Clay protesting annexation of Texas. Takes part in protest meeting at Faneuil Hall on behalf of Elizah Lovejoy.

1838 Publishes lecture on war. Signs petition on behalf of Abner Kneeland. Delivers lecture on "Self-Culture." Finds essential agreement with Emerson's Divinity School Address.

1839 "Remarks on Slavery Question," criticism of Henry Clay's attitude.

1840 Publishes lectures on "Elevation of the Laboring Classes" and on "Emancipation."

1841 Theodore Parker's sermon on "Transient and Permanent in Christianity." Channing accepts basic idea though critical of Parker's dismissal of miracles. Channing's works published in five volumes.

1842 Preaches for the last time at Federal Street on April 7. Publishes "Duty of the Free States" in two parts. Delivers Lenox Address on August 1, 1842. Dies on October 2 at Bennington, Vermont.

1843 Sixth volume of works published.

William Ellery Channing

CHAPTER 1

The Molding of a Man

WILLIAM ELLERY CHANNING was born on April 7, 1780, in Newport, Rhode Island, in the midst of the Revolutionary War. Nature had provided a birthplace of breath-taking beauty, but British troops had savagely laid it waste, denuding the land of trees and vegetation. Before the Revolution Newport had been a leading commercial center; poetry and romance clung to her spars and sails and brightened her somnolent days. But war had shrunk the population nearly in half at the time Channing was born, and his early years were spent among scenes of desolation only partially offset by the natural loveliness of land and sea.

William Ellery was the fourth child and third son of William Channing, attorney general of the state of Rhode Island, and of Lucy Ellery, daughter of one of the signers of the Declaration of Independence.[1] William Channing had entered the law after his graduation from Nassau Hall, Princeton, where his prosperous merchant father had sent him to receive a sound, conservative education. Philip Freneau, James Madison, Henry Brackenridge, and Henry Lee were classmates and friends destined to leave more lasting marks on the scroll of fame, although William Channing had become one of Rhode Island's most highly respected citizens and public officials. His father-in-law, William Ellery, was a Harvard man and one of the "Sons of Liberty," who served in the Continental Congress both before and after his grandson's birth. Between the two there was an intimacy even stronger than that of father and son.

The Channing children were sent early to school because their mother's health was poor. William, so young that he had to be carried by a colored servant, went from one dame school to another[2] until he was ready to attend the boarding school of Master Rogers, a local pedagogue whose reputation had spread beyond Newport and Rhode Island as well. If he used the rod unsparingly, he was neither worse nor better than any of his contemporaries.[3] At Rogers' school William learned his lessons well. He learned also to hate flogging, not so much for the pain as for the insult it offered to the spirit. Here too he became acquainted with young Malbone, a celebrated painter in later years, and Washington Allston, one of the cheery Southern lads who had been drawn to Newport by accounts of Master Rogers' school.

William was not considered quick in school. There is a story of his having had difficulty in Latin until an assistant in his father's office took pity on him and said, "Come, come Bill! They say you are a fool, but I know better; bring me your grammar and I will soon teach you Latin."[4] Whoever he was, the good lawyer must have possessed the divine afflatus, because "Bill" read the classics and especially Virgil with great delight in his college years. He also had encouragement and wise instruction from his grandfather, who loved the classics like vintage wine and never tired of discoursing upon the Ancients.

In the hours not devoted to school work, William enjoyed himself in the million and one pursuits that please the mind and body of an active boy. There was one prohibition, however, that his mother strictly enforced. She forbade her boys to bathe in the sea without supervision, and woe to him who disobeyed her. The combination of warm sun, inviting water, and dusty boy generally proving too much for childish wills, there were often culprits before the Channing bar of justice, but never William. According to his older brother George, William agreed to his mother's proposal to practice swimming on the kitchen table.[5] However free from danger such a method might be, it was singularly unsuccessful in teaching one to swim. William never learned; and, although he might have glowed with virtue because of his mother's wishes, he must have felt unhappy on the many occasions he had to walk home alone from the beach while his brothers and fellow playmates splashed happily in the surf.

The Rhode Island of Channing's youth was relatively iso-

lated. Southward she looked to the open sea and to gleaming
sails and spired masts. North, east, and west the placid waters
of Narragansett Bay laved softly against her shores. Glen and
cove called mysteriously to child and man alike. Craggy ledges
gave testimony to the fury of the sea but imperiously held
against its violence; and the beaches stretching out for miles
beside the blue sea beneath ever-changing skies and the
white sun made up a landscape of startling beauty. For the
growing child the only yardstick was the pleasure of the
moment, and the carefree boy could have only an intimation
of the immensity of nature's gifts. But one day the man would
realize that nothing on earth had helped to form his character
so much as the beauty of his early home.

William's later memories of the early years of Newport were
not entirely pleasant. His father was often too busy to spare
time for his son. Lawyer Channing was a strict disciplinarian
who followed the example of most parents of the period who
believed that children should be kept at a distance.[6] Still
there were rare occasions when he unbent enough to tell
the boy about old Nassau and of his hopes of one day sending
him there. More frequent than these informal talks were the
times when William went to court with his father. One of the
golden moments occurred when his father took him to the
State convention that adopted the Federal Constitution. There
he saw and heard Rhode Island patriots who were happy at
last to be a part of the union of states.

I Politics and Religion

More than most boys of his age William was keenly aware
of the political questions agitating the country. Grandfather
Ellery, who had returned to Congress the year after William's
birth, had remained there until the boy was seven. A Whig
during the revolution, he had become a Federalist after the
war, still following the banner of his idol Washington.[7] After
his retirement from Congress he returned to Newport; there
he molded the character of his grandson and printed indelibly
on the boy's mind principles to which he himself was devoted.
In the pursuit of truth, for example, the old man was always
more eager for certainty than for amount and variety of re-

sults. When the truth refused to give itself up to his search, he did not indulge in conjecture, nor did he expect the imperfect state of things always to produce certainty. In his own strong and characteristic manner of expression Grandfather Ellery held that the obligation to uphold liberty was just as sacred as that which bound him to his wife and children. Much of his fervor penetrated to the heart of his grandson, where it lay smoldering, ready to flame into passion whenever the cause of freedom was in danger of attack.

Lawyer Channing was also a devoted Federalist. At the beginning of the French Revolution, he shared in the universal hope for freedom; but, with the execution of Louis XVI, his hopes for France died and he turned to domestic affairs. As a leading lawyer and an earnest supporter of the Federal party, he was frequently asked to play host to eminent men. Washington dined at his home; and young William, who had never expected to see the great man face to face, had to be rescued from his hiding place under the table. John Jay and other noted men of the political world came to the Channing residence, and William had many opportunities to listen in on their councils. The world of politics, as a consequence, never ceased to fascinate him, even though he was seldom able to appreciate the merits of politicians themselves.

Matching his interest in politics was his concern for social evils. Intemperance impressed him as a really great evil. Drunken sailors stumbling aboard ship and intoxicated townsmen were common sights in Newport, but the boy's natural disgust was heightened by the contrast between the victims of rum and the sober persons of his father and grandfather. As for slavery, which he would later judge the most wicked of all human crimes, he seems to have been completely ignorant. The only explanation for his failure to recognize the evil of domestic slavery is that he had been taught that it was part of the normal scheme of things.

Slavery was familiar to him, for Negro servants waited on him at home. His grandfather, John, like most respectable merchants of Newport, had imported slaves from Africa; and Lawyer Channing never openly opposed the practice of keeping slaves. He did, however, liberate his own servants after the Revolution. One of them, Duchess, had a home of her own to which she often invited the children of the family whom she served. At such gatherings William learned that race and color were no bar to affection and honesty.

Not the least significant influence on William's childhood was the force of religion. His Grandfather Ellery, a student of ecclesiastical history and dogmatic divinity, was fond of discussing disputed points of theology although he abhorred sectarianism. He attended the Congregational church regularly but overcame any impulse he might have had to become a church member. Harmony among Christians, he believed, would be more readily achieved "if party names were entirely disused."[8]

William's father was a member of the Second Congregational Church; and Ezra Stiles, grandson of the Puritan poet Edward Taylor, was the family minister until called to the presidency of Yale. Stiles had been licensed to preach in 1773, but his brilliantly receptive mind was filled with the deism of the time until he was called to the ministry of the Newport Church two years after his ordination. During Channing's early youth and young manhood, Stiles exerted a greater influence on him than any other man, with the possible exception of Grandfather Ellery. The indignation that William felt whenever he saw any invasion of human rights, he himself attributed to the example and teaching of his scholarly mentor. No other being, he declared, excited as much reverence from him while Stiles was still alive.[9] What stirred him most about the older man was his lack of sectarian spirit. Stiles carried into his religious teaching and practice the same spirit of liberty which then animated the whole country politically.

Another man, in many ways the antithesis of Stiles, considerably influenced the youthful Channing. This was the Reverend Samuel Hopkins, whose doctrine of "Hopkinsianism" was to become a byword in the religious controversies of the coming century. His doctrine of "willingness to be damned for the sake of Christ," though abhorrent to the modern mind, became the badge of "consistent" Calvinists when "a foolish consistency" was the hobgoblin of very serious minds.

Channing's first impressions of Hopkins were unfavorable. Because his own church, the Second Congregational, was closed during his childhood, he accompanied his parents to Hopkins' services.[10] With an average share of the normal child's restlessness, he found little in Hopkins' appearance or message to attract him. Adding to his discomfort was the fact that the church was as cold as a barn in wintertime. Windows rattled and added their cacophony to the minister's raucous delivery. Hell-fire might prove a palatable diet for the spirit, but it had little effect on shivering bodies. So it was that William was introduced to the gaunt old minister and his stern diet.[11]

But William was to alter his opinion of Dr. Hopkins. Hopkins' fiery indictment of the local slave trade had earned him few friends in Newport, which cherished its West Indies traffic. Channing, however, did not forget the old man's benevolence, and in his total assessment of the man it outweighed the pervasive gloom of his doctrine.

And speaking of the gloom, it must be remembered that the prevailing winds of doctrine in Newport, as in the rest of New England, were Calvinistic although the specter of the Genevan reformer had already begun to lose its haunting force in the post-Revolutionary world. Though hell-fire and damnation might seem to youngsters like Channing to partake more of the nature of vaudeville than of Christian preaching, there was yet a kernel of interest which needed only the confirmation of parents to germinate into the fruit of belief.

On one occasion when William Channing could spare some time for his son, he took him to hear a preacher who was attracting considerable attention by his evangelism. Impressed by his father's interest in driving some miles to the meeting, young William drank in the speaker's words. And a bitter message it was, though couched in glowing rhetoric. In one sense, it was another harrowing of hell. The depravity of man, his helplessness before evil, and his reliance on the sovereignty of God were so vividly described that there seemed no need for a heaven and certainly no room for any place but hell. The boy walked from the meeting in the company of his father, and the very heaven seemed filled with the same gloom that lay on his spirit. "Sound doctrine, sir," his father replied to an acquaintance; and the boy said to himself, "It is all *true.*" Henceforth, he reflected, all true believers would have to relinquish earthly pursuits to prepare for the day of judgment.

They got into the chaise and began the trip homeward, each lost in his own thoughts, the boy not daring to speak to his father, whose silence he took to be the result of feelings similar to his own. But presently his father began to whistle; and, when they reached home, instead of calling the rest of the family to share the terrible knowledge, he calmly sat down to read his newspaper. William was not slow to grasp the explanation for his father's conduct. What he had heard was not true! The sense of relief was gratifying; but it was soon succeeded by a feeling of anger, for he felt he had been imposed upon. He resolved never to be fooled again by fine words.[12]

When Channing was twelve, he was sent to New London, Connecticut, to prepare for Harvard with his Uncle Henry. The Reverend Henry Channing was an ardent supporter of the evangelical movements of the time, and, according to his friend Ezra Stiles, no longer believed in the divinity of Christ.[13] Under his tutelage William was further emancipated from the Calvinistic tenets which his father's unconcern over the brimstone teaching of the Rhode Island evangelist had led him to question some years earlier.

The unexpected death of his father in September, 1793, thrust new responsibility upon the Channing family, but they met the crisis bravely; and William worked as never before to prepare for college. He passed the entrance exams in the following summer and entered Harvard in the fall of 1794.

II *At Harvard*

Harvard in 1794 bore little resemblance to today's institution. There were only 173 students when Channing entered, although the entrance examinations in Greek and Latin never lived up to their rumored strictness.[14] The course of studies was ruled over by the Reverend Joseph Willard and a supporting cast of three professors and three tutors, who labored mightily, if not always effectively, to fill the "empty Sculls of young Harvards" with the classics, Watts' logic, and Locke's essays.

Though the curriculum was classical, there was small Latin and less Greek. According to Joseph Story, Channing's strongest rival for class honors, the number of textbooks probably did not exceed fifteen.[15] And from reports of Story, Sidney Willard, and Channing, the majority of the courses were textbook courses which allowed little latitude for either student or teacher. The students were required to memorize the rules in Blair's *Lectures on Rhetoric* and to recite orally the definitions in Lowth's *English Grammar*. Mathematics, which was not required for admission, proved rough going for nearly all. Logic was studied in the sophomore year. In the junior and senior years there were lectures on natural philosophy, accompanied by experiments. Attendance upon these was voluntary and there were no examinations. Lectures on astronomy came during the senior year, and the two-volume edition of the famous "Geography" by Jedidiah Morse, who would be one of Channing's most ardent opponents during the "unitarian" controversy some twenty years later, was used to supplement Euclid's *Elements*.

Not a diversified curriculum, but there was the college library to supplement course work. History and literature were Channing's favorite reading.[16] History being to him, as it was later to Carlyle, the biographies of great men, he read avidly books like *Demosthenes*. In literature he showed an unoriginal but catholic taste, dividing his time between the ancients and moderns. Of the latter, Bacon, Dryden, and Goldsmith pleased him equally. He was enthusiastic about Shakespeare, but the sprightly comedies of Colley Cibber and the family tragedies of George Lillo were also to his liking. His taste for Lillo's works is evidence that his sentimental appreciation of writers like Letitia Barbauld, Catherine Sedgwick, Joanna Baillie, and Mary Mitford was fostered at Harvard.

He was particularly interested in improving his speaking and writing. He read Longinus, Demosthenes, Sheridan, and Harris so that he might study elocution as an art; and he had easy access to the works of Blair, Campbell, and Lord Kames. He knew Blair by heart, and he was quite familiar with the pleasure-pain calculus of Lord Kames.

His deepest interest lay in books about man's spiritual nature. He carefully studied the works of John Locke, Bishop

Berkeley, Thomas Reid, David Hume, Joseph Priestley, and especially Richard Price. But Locke's empiricism and sensational psychology repelled him, and he welcomed an antidote in the writings of Price. Price's idealism saved him from Locke's sensationalism.[17] According to his own admission, Price's *Morals* and *Four Dissertations* molded his philosophy into its permanent form.

At Harvard, Channing also discovered the Edinburgh Enlightenment. Through Professor David Tappan and Harvard in general, he discovered Francis Hutcheson and his theory of benevolence and then the other Scottish liberals.[18] While reading Hutcheson's *Inquiry* one day in his favorite retreat, he came upon the doctrine of an innate moral sense and the theory of disinterested benevolence. The effect upon him was similar to that described by Jonathan Edwards in his *Personal Narrative*. As Channing later told a friend, "I longed to die, and felt as if heaven alone could give room for the exercise of such emotions; but when I found I must live, I cast about to do something worthy of these great thoughts. . . ."[19] From this time on, he remained convinced that altruism rather than self-love provided the only suitable motive for human beings living in a world of order and beauty.

Hutcheson revealed to him the infinite possibilities in man, but Adam Ferguson suggested to him that regeneration is a gradual and a social process. Later Channing discovered a more pleasing combination of Ferguson's secularism and Hutcheson's benevolence in Price's *Dissertations*. In all of these discoveries, he was guided by the hand of Levi Hedge, who was devoted to the Scottish school of common sense of which Thomas Brown, Thomas Reid, and Dugald Stewart were leading exponents.

Since Channing lived at the home of his Uncle Francis Dana instead of in one of the college dormitories, he escaped most of the unpleasant features of campus life; and the physical separation was no impediment to his social success. Though not really gregarious, he was one of four students in his class to belong to four major clubs: Phi Beta Kappa, the Porcellian, the Speaking Club, and Hasty Pudding. Among his small circle of friends, only three or four could really be considered intimate and perhaps the closest of all was his Newport companion, Washington Allston, who was already dreaming of becoming America's "first painter."[20]

Looking back years later at his college experiences, Channing recalled that Harvard "was never in a worse state than when I entered. . . . The French Revolution had diseased the imagination and unsettled the understanding of men everywhere. . . . The tendency of all classes was to skepticism."[21] Although Channing's indictment is extreme—perhaps because of his conservative political and religious beliefs as an undergraduate—influences from abroad did insinuate their way into the Harvard Yard although the campus was fairly isolated from world culture. Among these, deism and French infidelity gave serious people most reason to ponder how baneful their effects might be on immature minds.

In general, deism was a kind of lowest common denominator in religion. In its early stages reason and the beliefs to which it led were considered sufficient by the deists to enable man to know that God existed; that He ought to be worshiped through virtue and piety; that man ought to be sorry for sin and repent; and that divine goodness could reward and punish man in this world and the next according to his actions.[22] Later, Newtonian science provided deism with a divine architect operating through immutable laws while Lockean psychology through its empiricism fostered the deists' system of hedonistic ethics. Deism was now prepared to move and the appearance of Paine's *Age of Reason* in 1794 signaled the beginning of a direct offensive against religion and clerical authority. Harvard and other American colleges retaliated by equipping their students with Bishop Watson's *Apology for the Bible*, a standard rebuttal to Paine.[23]

Adding to the frenzy against the deists was the rising tide of hatred against France, a political enemy particularly obnoxious to New England Federalists, who lumped Jeffersonian Republicans, deists, and French infidels into one ball of intense dislike. "French infidelity" was simply deism clothed in nationalistic garments.[24]

The contagion of party feeling could not be kept outside the walls of Harvard. In his senior year Channing got permission to call a meeting to discuss the political crisis. At the meeting he spoke so eloquently that his classmates accepted his motion to send a message to President Adams. A committee to draw up the address was appointed, but Channing wrote most of the document that was finally sent to the president. A glance at the contents reveals that William was in complete accord with the sentiments of the party to which William Ellery and William Channing had been devoted. Glowing with patriotism and couched in typical eighteenth-century grandiloquence, William's effort was largely descriptive and rhetorical. One passage suffices to characterize its general tone and method: "We have seen a nation in Europe grasping at universal conquest, trampling on the laws of God and nations; systematizing rapine and plunder, destroying foreign governments by the strength of her arms or the pestilence of her embraces. . . . We have seen this same nation violating our neutral rights, spurning our pacific proposals, her piratical citizens sweeping our ships from the seas, and venal presses under her control pouring out torrents of abuse on men who have grown gray in our service. We have seen her ministers in this country insulting our government by a daring, unprecedented, and contemptuous appeal to the people. . . . We have seen this, Sir, and our youthful blood has boiled within us. . . . Our lives are our only property; and we were not the sons of those who sealed our liberties with their blood, if we would not defend with these lives that soil which now affords a peaceful grave to the mouldering bones of our forefathers."[25]

At Commencement Channing took as his subject, "The Present Age," when he was chosen to give the valedictory. Despite faculty efforts to avoid the partisan strife that had plagued previous commencements by prohibiting the introduction of party questions into student addresses, Channing won enough concessions from President Willard to deal with his topic as he saw fit. The enthusiastic response of an audience grateful for his stirring defense of free expression rang in his ears as he concluded his four years under the Harvard elms.

III *The Alien South*

After graduation Channing returned to his family in Newport, where he spent the summer. At first content to wander on the beach or visit friends and neighbors, he later became disquieted because he was uncertain about his future and had no prospects of immediate employment. Fortunately, he met David Randolph of Richmond, the United States marshal for Virginia, who offered him a job as tutor to his children. Channing accepted gladly and went to Richmond in the fall.

Southern society was a revelation. Famous visitors like John Marshall came to the Randolph home, and Channing was captivated by the generosity of Virginians and their open-hearted way of dealing with one another. Since the slave quarters were open for inspection, he took advantage of every opportunity to talk to the Negroes who worked on the Randolph and neighboring estates. Their wretchedness and the demoralizing effects of the system on all concerned, owner and slave alike, aroused his sympathy although he could not visualize even the beginnings of a solution. Nature, he was sure, had never made the distinction between black and white.[26]

Politically his new environment was even more alien to New England than socially. Newport and Cambridge were Federalistic; Virginia was Jeffersonian. Reared in places sacred to the memory of "Saint George" and among people devoted to the cause of Adams and the Constitution, Channing was now in the center of America's domestic Jacobins. The change in political climate was greater even than the difference between the wintry blasts of Maine and the zephyrs of Virginia, but it was a change that he needed. Federalism was only one side of the political coin, and his vision of reforming and instructing a vicious and ignorant world required a whole view of the universe. He was still quite firmly opposed to Jacobinism, but his attitude toward France had softened.

Notwithstanding some chinks in his political armor, Channing's Federalism was still tolerably sound. The day was yet far off when his liberalism would merit the name of "loco-foco."[27] He was still happy to find "odium . . . everywhere attached to the name of Jacobin" and he replied "implicitly on the firmness and independence of the president" to frustrate the machinations of the French. He wished "France to fall," but he did not want England "to rise on her ruins."

Dreaming of social improvement projected by radical French thinkers and their English followers, he decided to undertake a systematic course of study. He read Hume but found that he did not "throw light enough on the rest of Europe." After wondering whether he must "wade through Gibbon to get acquainted with the Empire," he finally decided to postpone the "Decline" to another time. Ferguson's "Civil Society" proved a delightful replacement. From William Robertson he discovered "a right direction in historical matters," but *Eloise* turned out to be more exciting. He wrote Shaw, "Rousseau is the only French author I have ever read, who knows the way to the heart." Turning from Jean Jacques, he devoured William Godwin's *Caleb Williams,* although his *Political Justice* was also a favorite. He could not agree with Godwin's mechanistic universe or with his favoring reason to the exclusion of man's emotions, but he did seize upon the idea that all "human inventions are capable of perpetual improvement."

Writing to William Shaw early in 1799, he outlined his views of how man should be enfranchised. Avarice was the chief obstacle to human progress, he declared. The only way to eliminate it was to establish a community of property. Convinced that virtue and benevolence were natural to man, he blamed selfishness and greed upon the false ideas of superiority of the body over the mind and the separation of individual interest from that of the community as a whole. Men must be educated to understand that the powers and dignity of their minds were unlimited. To this end he sketched, in his letters to Shaw and Arthur Walter, another Harvard classmate, a scheme for a fraternal organization that would have as its goal the foundation of human happiness. His friends thought him crazy and spoke laughingly of his grandiose ideas.

Arthur Walter, pretending with mock seriousness to accept his scheme, proposed to carry out the "imaginary republic of Coleridge and Southey, and a community of goods, in the backwoods, or better far, in some South-sea island." Francis Channing reminded him of Plato and Socrates and of their utopian projects, and then added: "My brother advances with noble ardor to a vaster enterprise. . . . To make all men happy, by making all virtuous, in his glorious project. I adore it, thou moral Archimedes! But where wilt thou stand to move the mental world?"[28]

IV Sense of Duty

Channing had come to Virginia to support himself while preparing for the ministry. Since his tutoring duties were not demanding, he had time for study; but he nearly ruined his health by staying up most of the night, sleeping on the bare floor, and going without proper clothing in the day. Physical weakness led to dyspepsia and idle fancies, which in turn aroused his passions. As he confessed to Shaw, "I sit down with Goldsmith or Rogers in my hand, and shed tears— at what? At fictitious misery; at tales of imaginary woe."[29] Not long after, the lack of relation between benevolence and feeling dawned upon him. Tears might flow and misery remain unchecked, or one might charge "the cavalry of woe" within and no one ever know or care.

Virtue, he decided, was not feeling; it meant "acting from a sense of duty."[30] Here, for the first time, was a full realization of what was meant by the "innate moral sense" of Shaftesbury, Hutcheson, and Price. And it led shortly after to "A change of heart," as he called it, that fits the classic description of orthodox Calvinist conversion. Morality appeared now to be only "a branch from the vigorous root of religion" and the Bible to be "the only source of divine knowledge."[31] To seal his new-found covenant, he penned an act of self-consecration, laying bare past offenses and promising sincerely to seek God's love and justice.

He had come to Virginia filled with political enthusiasm and believing that pure morality, or "disinterested benevolence," was sufficient to secure human happiness and to open up the way to unlimited progress. Now his political liberalism had deepened into religious faith, and his secular morality had received a large infusion of religious piety. As a matter of fact, his sense of piety was in kind and degree not very dissimilar from that of Jonathan Edwards. In time, however, Edwardean piety would gradually disappear; and he would love mankind for its dynamic potential of human goodness.

The transition would be final when it occurred, but the time was still years away.

After he had been with the Randolphs for a year and a half, he asked them to release him because his health demanded complete rest and quiet. They agreed, and he left Richmond for Newport in July. His family could scarcely recognize the pallid invalid who greeted them at the dock. Gone was the smiling and vigorous youngster, and in his place stood an old-young man who was a stranger. Had they fully comprehended the changes in him, they would have been more dismayed; for he was mentally and spiritually far removed from the boy who had charmed their hearts with gay banter.

While William was convalescing, he kept busy by tutoring young Randolph, who had returned with him from Richmond, and his own brother, Edward Tyrrel. He drew up a list of suggestions for self-discipline, and heading the list was an injunction to cultivate an active spirit of Christian charity. Religion, he reminded himself, must never be represented as gloomy or hopeless. Charity demanded that he respect all sects no matter how he might differ, but "it will sometimes be necessary to change the tone of approbation and pity to that of denial."[32]

In the quiet precincts of the Redwood Library he spent days and sometimes weeks without interruption. When he grew tired of his peaceful study, he went to the beach where the roar of the surf and the brilliant sunshine combined to restore his energies. If these two favorite haunts were influential in shaping his mind, the friendship of the seventy-year-old Samuel Hopkins was even more important. William had never really become acquainted with the old gentleman until now, but soon he began to look forward with increasing eagerness to his visits to the gambrel-roofed parsonage of Dr. Hopkins. The fact that Hopkins not only preached but practiced his theory of disinterested benevolence attracted William despite his horror of Hopkins' views that man was predestined and should be willing to be damned if God so destined.

Hopkins' system contained a number of paradoxes. Although he accepted the most severe form of predestination, he rejected the doctrines of total depravity and election; and this action led Channing in later years to give Hopkins full credit for "mitigating the harsh features" of the Genevan system; but it was Hopkins' idea of benevolence that really thrilled Channing. For the first time, its image became clear and distinct in his mind and soul. Hutcheson had developed, Price had enlarged, and Samuel Hopkins had printed the finished picture that now lay before him.

In December, 1801, Channing was appointed a Regent at Harvard. Leaving Newport, he arrived in Cambridge in January, 1802, to assume his new duties. The office was little more than a sinecure but he was thankful because his new position provided him with financial support and the resources of the Harvard Library. In the Harvard Yard he buckled down to the serious study of divinity. President Willard and Professor Tappan were available for advice, but Channing worked pretty much by himself. His reading, as evidenced by a recommended list he gave years afterward to a friend, was confined largely to English divines since the German era of scientific theology had not yet dawned in America.[33]

In general he thought little of English theology and considered the established church "the grave of intellect" and "a dozing place to minds which anywhere else would have signalized themselves." Even so he admitted there were "powerful thinkers" in the English church and made up a reading list headed by Butler's *Analogy* and *Sermons*. Then followed books on miracles, the reasonableness of Christianity, freedom of the will, and the psychology of man. Although he omitted Hooker, Cudworth, and Chillingworth of the Cambridge school, his bent was everywhere away from books emphasizing materialistic and utilitarian views.

Of the writers most frequently mentioned (i.e., in addition to Hutcheson, Ferguson, and Price), Joseph Butler and William Law came first. Butler's sermons "Upon Human Nature" he regarded as unsurpassed in English. Law appealed to his sympathies because of a piety that approached mysticism. His interest in these two authors, so unlike in most ways and representing divergent currents of mind in the intellectual climate of the Enlightenment, shows his capacity for entertaining the claims of both the rationalists and the intuitionists. Like his pupil and successor, Emerson, he possessed a dualism reminiscent of the early Puritans, who not only studied Ramean logic but also sought out God's "wonder-working providences."

The habit of self-examination begun in Newport was continued at Harvard. He was aware that he read too much and reflected too little, and he resolved to reverse the procedure by concentrating on primary sources of knowledge. Most evident among his self-admonitions is the tone of humility. Though never entirely lacking, it had now become almost childlike. Noteworthy also was the change in his studies. He had pushed secular knowledge into the background so that he could concentrate on the Bible. Already he had begun to lay the foundation for the criticisms of him as a man of narrow scope and limited depth. But the improvement of the heart struck him as infinitely more important than the enlargement of the understanding.

As he neared the end of his studies, he joined the First Church in Cambridge, under the charge of Dr. Abiel Holmes, the father of Oliver Wendell Holmes and a Yale graduate but "liberal—for a Connecticut man." In the autumn of 1802 he appeared before the Cambridge Association and was approved to preach after satisfying one questioner concerning his views on the authorship of sin. He gave his first sermon in Medford on October 24, 1802, and chose for his text, "Silver and gold, have I none, but such as I have I give thee." Subsequent sermons on the same subject of benevolence were so successful that he received invitations to settle with two Boston churches, the congregations at Brattle Street and Federal Street. On February 12, 1803, he accepted the latter because he thought it would make fewer demands upon his health. He was ordained on June 1, 1803. Abiel Holmes gave the introductory prayer; Henry Channing delivered the charge; and David Tappan delivered the ordination sermon. Moderates in theology, their presence was proof of Channing's growing sympathies for a less severe religion than old-guard Calvinism.

For the first few months after his settlement Channing was too preoccupied with personal problems to give much thought to the world around him. Though never the recluse that Nathaniel Hawthorne later became, he was guilty of the same heinous fault for which Hawthorne's Ethan Brand had searched so unsuccessfully. Unlike Brand, who discovered too late that the unpardonable sin was "the sin of an intellect that triumphed over the sense of brotherhood with man and reverence for God, and sacrificed everything to its own mighty claims," Channing, whose moral nature was more highly developed, realized in time that his "speculations about the origin of moral feelings, etc., cannot justify a practical neglect of them."[34]

Most of his troubles were due to overscrupulousness that made him feel unworthy to carry on God's work. But that was only part of the answer. He was convinced that he and all other men were sinful by nature; and, although he himself had had little actual experience of sin, he had inherited a strong sense of personal guilt. More accurately perhaps, his association with Hopkins, an inveterate searcher after personal faults, had aroused a latent scrupulosity. It took some frank talk from his older brother to straighten out his thinking and bring him to his senses.

From the beginning his preaching proved successful. He stated his beliefs with an earnestness and sincerity that could not fail to impress his listeners. Believing man infinitely perfectible with a moral faculty capable of being unfolded, much as the intellectual capacities are capable of development, he preached virtue as the true end of religion and government.[35] All men, he declared, must be aware of their duties and obligations to each other, to their community, and to their nation. His duty was to assist and guide them. Perhaps the chief novelty in his preaching was the directness with which he brought his Christian principles to bear upon actual life. His limited resources were a handicap; but he did what he could by lending books, encouraging study groups, and discussing whatever problems his parishioners chose to bring him. His parishioners, both young and old, were impressed by the intimacy with which he dealt in the sermons with matters of fact at the same time that he reached above them to explain the glory of God's word.

When the first number of *The Monthly Anthology* appeared, he was listed as a contributor. His short moral fable, "The Guest," conveyed old sentiments in a new guise. Stylistically barren of the flesh-and-blood detail of sound narrative, it was too didactic to win readers by its artistic merits. In addition there were several other short pieces, one of which, in language reminiscent of Carlyle, anticipated the philosophy of *Sartor Resartus* by remarking that "dress, like the countenance, is an expression of the soul."[36]

If these early attempts at literary composition are to be fairly judged, it must be admitted that they do not reveal any specific talent; but they were neither better nor worse than the other contributions to *The Anthology*. More ambitious attempts would not be made until many years later, when a more polished style—the result of writing and delivering hundreds of sermons and public addresses—would earn acclaim for the famous "Dr. Channing."

V *Theological Warfare*

During the spring following Channing's literary debut, his Uncle Henry was dismissed by his own congregation. After twenty years of service, a church council had found him sufficiently lacking in orthodox beliefs to relieve him of his duties. In Connecticut, tolerance of heresy was narrower than in Massachusetts; but the events of the next few years would prove tolerance far from excessive in the Bay State also. To begin with, there were three fairly distinct parties in the established Congregational order of Massachusetts. In the center were the moderates: men like Abiel Holmes, David Tappan, and Joseph Buckminster of Portsmouth, who were only slightly influenced either by the new-light doctrines of Jonathan Edwards on the right or by the liberalism of left-wingers like John Kirkland and William Bentley, the fabulous Salem diarist. To the right were the "consistent" Calvinists, followers of Samuel Hopkins.

On the left were the liberals, the smallest of the three groups and strong only in Boston and its environs. For the most part Harvard-trained, this group rejected Calvinism. Among their number were William Emerson, Joseph Tuckerman, young Buckminster, and many of Channing's friends. He, however, was still not a member of any of the groups. Although he had rejected the main doctrines of Calvinism and was certainly unorthodox in his Christology, traces of Samuel Hopkins' influence still lingered despite his small sympathy for Hopkins' followers.

The growing tensions among the three parties came to a climax in 1805 with the establishment by the orthodox of an argumentative periodical, the *Panoplist,* and with the affair known as the Harvard Controversy. Jedidiah Morse, the moving spirit behind the *Panoplist,* was trying desperately to guard the orthodox citadel against liberals like Buckminster, John Kirkland, and William Emerson; he was ready, therefore, to do battle with any and all whom he considered guilty of contaminating the pure stream of evangelical teaching. Morse was aching for a showdown, and the appointment of the Hollis Professor of Divinity at Harvard gave him an excellent opportunity.

The liberals supported Henry Ware, Sr. and the conservatives favored Jesse Appleton. The former, against whom charges of Arminianism and Unitarianism were leveled by the orthodox, was supported by Judge Francis Dana, Channing's uncle. Ware finally was elected; and for Jedidiah Morse, the election was an incentive. A true heresy-hunter, he would not stop until he had stirred up a tempest that would engulf Channing in the next decade.[37]

Although Channing exchanged pulpits freely with both orthodox and liberals, his evangelical sentiments showed a leaning to the former. For example, at the ordination of John Codman in 1808 when describing the duties of a minister to his congregation, he painted a word-picture of "that fire which is never quenched, of that worm which never dies."[38] He was at this time an Edwards without the poetic fire but with the technique of drawing the sinner so close to the abyss that he would have cause to repent and seek holiness. And yet, Channing was gradually abandoning this approach as he began to formulate his ideas more clearly.

If the idea of God's paternity had not succeeded that of Divine Sovereignty, it was beginning to seem very attractive. In his journal he wrote: "I do not perceive that we dishonor God by believing that his creation is a real source of felicity to him, that he finds a real happiness in doing good, and in viewing with complacence obedient, virtuous, and happy children."³⁹ Although this idea is pure anthropomorphism, Channing saw nothing specious in comparing divine and human perfection. Though not prepared to equate them, he was nevertheless working steadily toward the idea of "essential sameness," which would set his theology apart from that of Protestant and Catholic theologians alike.⁴⁰ Furthermore, he was defecting from the traditional view of the atonement. "Mercy," he declares, "is an essential attribute of God, not an affection produced in him by a foreign cause."⁴¹ As for his Christology, he was an Arian rather than a Socinian: he believed Christ to be more than human but still less than God.

Channing's life during the years when he was still unknown beyond the immediate Boston area was rather uneventful. He lived happily in the parsonage on Berry Street with his mother and her family and bided his time until he could marry. He was grieved by the premature death of his older brother in 1810, and two years later, by that of his friend and rival, Joseph Buckminster. With his former pupil Samuel Thacher, Channing undertook the job of editing Buckminster's sermons for publication. His own reputation, somewhat overshadowed in the past by that of Buckminster, now began to spread as increasing numbers of people came to the new Federal Street Church that had been built in 1809 to accommodate them.

On July 21, 1814, he married his childhood playmate and cousin Ruth Gibbs. After the years at Harvard and Richmond, Channing had seen Ruth only occasionally in Newport and Boston, but he had never questioned how he felt about her although he could not speak of love until he felt able to support her and was sure that she loved him. Her wealth was always a matter of scruple to him; but after his marriage he contentedly lived on Beacon Street and spent his summers at "Oakland," the family estate near Portsmouth, Rhode Island. But his manner of living remained almost ascetic, as it always had been.

As the first decade of his ministry came to an end, Channing was honored by an appointment to deliver the Dexter Lectures on Biblical Criticism at Harvard. He had recently become chairman of the executive committee of the Bible Society of Massachusetts, and he was the obvious choice to receive the post left vacant by Joseph Buckminster's death. His plans were ambitious, for he bought many of the books Buckminster had acquired in his travels abroad and settled down to serious preparation; but poor health forced him to resign within the year. He did, however, accept membership on the Harvard Corporation, a responsibility he discharged until 1825.

What positive effects might have resulted from Channing's continuing as a lecturer can only be speculated about. Certainly a firsthand acquaintance with German philosophy would not have changed his basic mind-set: the pattern of his thinking was pretty well determined, and he had long been familiar with the doctrine of idealism. His becoming a scholar like his successor, Andrews Norton, was highly improbable, both because he feared scholarship might lead to cultivating the understanding at the expense of the emotions and also because his mind was essentially synthetic rather than analytic, intuitive rather than critical.

Despite his never robust health Channing was giving more and more attention to public affairs. When Napoleonic conquest was at its height, he chided fellow Bostonians for their apathy toward the fate of other nations; when war with Britain broke out, he called it unjustified, although he granted that the United States had serious provocation. "The cry has been," he said, "that war is declared, and all opposition should therefore be hushed. A sentiment more unworthy of a free country can hardly be propagated: War more than any other measure of a government should be subject to free discussion by the people."[42] But he was in disagreement with his Federalist friends; and, while he found much to praise in Federalism, he was obliged to admit that the "party in some respects failed of its duty to the cause of the Union and of Freedom."[43] Its failure, however, was due not to treachery but to despondency: its leaders had the "wisdom of experience" but lacked the "wisdom of hope."[44]

At war's end, his sermon of thanksgiving expressed the general sentiments of most Americans, who looked forward to peace and prosperity. As the *Columbian Sentinel* told its readers, it was now an "era of good feeling," and patriots should work together toward peace and prosperity. President Madison's message to Congress in 1815 breathed the same note of optimism and even contained a note of conciliation to uncooperative Federalists.

Peace among nations and "good feeling" might be called for, but precious little of either prevailed among the various religious factions in and around Boston in 1815. The rift had been widening for some time. Hopkinsians had joined uneasily with Old Calvinists in 1808 to establish Andover Seminary as protection against the growing "infidelity" at Harvard. Channing's friend, John Codman, had refused exchange with liberal ministers shortly after his ordination, and Jedidiah Morse and Samuel Miller of the Princeton Seminary had supported him. According to William Bentley of Salem, "Morse and Co. had contemplated a Union, a Consociation of Churches. . . ."[45] For Nathanael Emmons, the leading Hopkinsian of the day, this was too horrible to contemplate: "Association leads to Consociation, Consociation to Presbyterianism, Presbyterianism to Episcopalianism, and Episcopalianism to Popery."[46] His words wrote an end to further attempts at combining congregations.

But Morse and his followers had persisted in their attack upon the liberals. In their mouthpiece, the *Panoplist,* they had called for "ecclesiastical tribunals" to search out heresy; and they had so aroused their opponents that Channing was himself forced into writing Noah Worcester, editor of a religious magazine and a man of liberal views, an invitation to come to Boston to edit a new periodical that would teach Christians their Christian rights and awaken them to a firmer attachment to Christian liberty.[47] Worcester had accepted, and the *Christian Disciple* was born in 1813 with Channing as a leading contributor. After Worcester had begun his editorship, Morse had needled the liberals until he drew blood.[48]

If his intention had been to force the liberals into the open, he succeeded by jabbing their egos with a reprint of Thomas Belsham's chapter on American Unitarianism, which had appeared three years earlier in London as part of the English dissenter's *Memoirs of the Life of the Rev. Theophilus Lindsey.* The information concerning the American churches was innocuous; but Morse prefaced the thirty-eight pages from

Belsham's work with ten of his own which insinuated an identification between the Boston liberals and the English Unitarian. A favorable review of Morse's pamphlet by Jeremiah Evarts, editor of the *Panoplist,* appeared in the June, 1815, issue. It acted like a lighted fuse dropped in a keg of powder. Its purpose was three-fold: to identify American liberals with English Unitarians; to convict the former of dishonesty in concealing their Unitarian opinions; and to demand the exclusion of all Unitarians from Christian courtesy and fellowship.

The resulting explosion rocked Boston Congregationalism to its foundations. Even Channing with his deep-seated opposition to controversy was moved. His defense was *A Letter to the Rev. Samuel C. Thacher, on the Aspersions contained in a Late Number of The Panoplist, on the Ministers of Boston and the Vicinity.* In it he categorically denied that the Liberal Christians were in agreement with the materialistic, necessitarian, Socinian doctrine of Belsham. The second part of Channing's rebuttal was of greater importance than the first, for it answered his opponents' assertion that Liberal Christians "are guilty of hypocritical concealment of their sentiments; behave in a base, cowardly and hypocritical manner." To this charge, he replied: "We have only followed a general system, which we are persuaded to be best for our people and for the cause of Christianity; the system of excluding controversy as much as possible from our pulpits."[49] He concluded by expressing the hope that unity might be restored to all Christian churches since "error of opinion is an evil too trifling to be named in comparison with this practical departure from the gospel."[50]

Samuel Worcester, younger brother of the editor of the *Christian Disciple,* undertook to answer Channing's *Letter* in a series of three pamphlets, two of which Channing answered.[51] Both men held irreconcilable views about the Trinity and the atonement; and when Channing realized there was no point of agreement, he withdrew from the controversy and prepared *The System of Exclusion and Denunciation in Religion Considered,* a statement of principles published in 1815.[52] Meanwhile, other liberals joined in the controversy; and one of these, John Lowell, uncle of the poet and

Boston's leading political authority, published a pamphlet entitled *Are You a Christian or a Calvinist?* His attack offended many, but it was an excellent rejoinder to another question that had been stealthily making the rounds: "Are you of the Boston or the Christian Religion?" To Lowell, the quarrel looked like a fight between Massachusetts and Connecticut, between Harvard and Yale; and he attributed the acrimony of the orthodox (Yale men mostly, with some from the College of New Jersey) to jealousy of the University of Cambridge which "yields to no other seminary in our country."[53]

During the next several years the conflict continued with laymen taking their turn at pamphlet warfare and ministers having their say in the annual Convocation Sermons. For the most part, the liberals were merely defensive; but in the spring of 1819 a counteroffensive was launched with Baltimore as the testing ground. The occasion was the ordination of Jared Sparks—a young friend of Channing—who was now about to become minister of the First Independent Church in Baltimore, a city still very much in the control of an orthodox ministry. For his ordination speaker Sparks had chosen Channing and was rewarded by an address, nearly an hour and a half long, entitled "Unitarian Christianity." In it Channing presented a full exposition of the liberals' position—their belief in the unity of God and the unity of Christ; their emphasis upon the moral perfection of God and the moral nature of man; and their insistence upon human reason in interpreting the Scriptures.[54]

The Baltimore sermon pleased Northern liberals in the same measure that it horrified Northern and Southern conservatives alike; one of the latter called it "modified deism" and a system "infidels everywhere prefer." And as usual, it precipitated further pamphlet warfare. Professor Moses Stuart of Andover published *Letters to the Rev. Wm. E. Channing* and was answered by Andrews Norton's *A Statement of Reasons for Not Believing the Doctrines of Trinitarians.* Both men were competent scholars, but neither could gain an advantage.

Another stage in the controversy was developed through the exchange of pamphlets by Dr. Leonard Woods of Andover, a good friend of Jedidiah Morse, and Henry Ware, Sr.[55] The Wood n' Ware controversy, as it came to be known, was conducted on a high plane over the classical doctrines of depravity, election, and reprobation; but again the result left both combatants with unchanged points of view. The debate dragged into the 1830's but with rising emotions among the orthodox especially after the Unitarian-dominated Massachusetts Supreme Court in 1820 handed down its "Dedham decision," a ruling giving all property rights to the members of a parish who remained when there had been a separation in the congregation. Since the orthodox were usually the separatists, most of the Churches were soon in Unitarian hands. Jedidiah Morse called this maneuver "plundering," but it was legal.[56]

Although Channing did not enter directly into the controversy, he defended Unitarianism against the charge of being "a half-way house to infidelity" in an article in *The Christian Disciple* in 1819, and a year later in the same magazine his *Moral Argument Against Calvinism* underscored his distaste for views that falsified the nature of the deity. As in his sermon *Unitarian Christianity Most Favorable to Piety,* preached at the dedication of the Second Unitarian Church of New York on December 7, 1826, and also in the Election Sermon of 1830, which seemed so noble to Emerson, Channing emphasized in these publications his unfaltering faith in the moral and rational foundations of the universe.

There were, of course, tribulations to test his confidence in God's right order. In 1815, his sister Ann, who was married to Washington Allston, had died; the next year his own first-born had also died. Four years later his grandfather, William Ellery, had died just short of his ninety-third year. But there was profit as well as loss in the accounting: his daughter Mary, born in 1818, and his sons George and William, born in 1820 and 1821, respectively, were sources of fatherly pride and cause for thanksgiving.

So, too, was Harvard's award of an honorary doctor of divinity degree for Channing's services to the community in 1820. About the same time he was invited—but declined—to become minister of the First Congregational Society of New York. The events of the past few years had taken such a heavy toll from his never robust physique that he decided in the summer of 1821 to forsake his usual visit to Rhode Island in favor of a trip to the mountains of New Hampshire and Vermont. The sojourn was exhilarating but did him such little good physically that he agreed to turn over his pulpit temporarily to the young Orville Dewey in order to make plans for a trip abroad.

VI   *European Experiences*

On May 26, 1822, the Sunday before he was due to sail, he told his congregation that he was torn between his sense of duty to them and his anticipation of the pleasure he would derive from "traversing countries which have kindled my imagination almost from infancy, whose literature has been the food of my mind, and where nature and society present aspects hardly to be conceived amidst the freshness of our own institutions."[57] The next day he and his wife sailed for England.

The voyage across the Atlantic was uneventful, for Channing was confined to his cabin most of the time. He wrote in his journal, "Nature breathes nothing unkind. It expands, or calms, or softens us. . . . The soul and nature are attuned together. Something within answers to all we witness without." This exquisite correspondence between nature and the human soul had never before been so manifest to him. Like Emerson later, he was thoroughly convinced that "the axioms of physics translate the laws of ethics."

Upon arrival in Liverpool the Channings were warmly greeted, but they set off for the Lake Country as soon as possible to view scenes they had only read about but more particularly to visit Channing's idol, Wordsworth. Wordsworth had long been a favorite, although the spirit of the man and his philosophy rather than his skill as an author attracted Channing. From his first reading of the *Lyrical Ballads,* he had been impressed by the poet's love of man and the piety of his poems. Shortly after *The Excursion* was published, he had obtained a copy of it and "never read anything but Shakespeare more."

He found Wordsworth at home and received a cordial

welcome. They chatted about poetry and religion, and Channing warmed to his favorite argument that Christianity "contained nothing which rendered it unadapted to a progressive state of society. . . ."[58] Wordsworth read from a manuscript of *The Prelude* passages illustrating his doctrine of communion with Nature as a part of human development.

The following day he met the poet laureate, Robert Southey, whose defense of Anglicanism was too much for Channing to stomach. Leaving London in the middle of August, the Channings went to Paris. After several weeks there, they traveled leisurely through the French countryside toward the Swiss border; and from Geneva in late September Channing wrote his sister-in-law Susan: "All that nature can do to lift us above the sordid and selfish is done in Switzerland; and who can doubt that where there is a deep purpose in the soul to elevate itself, much aid may be derived from the sublimity of the external world?"[59]

Winter found the two in Italy. In Florence the wonders of European art exceeded Channing's anticipations, but nothing struck him more than "the apparent insensibility of the mass of the people to the masterpieces; and the fact, that in the churches, side by side with these masterpieces, were the most miserable modern daubs and images of the Virgin adorned with tinsel."[60]

When the Channings reached Rome in the middle of December, they received the shocking news of twin deaths in their immediate family. Although they were deeply grieved to learn of the death of their sister-in-law, Barbara Channing, the news of the death of their youngest child left them brokenhearted. Hurrying home as fast as health and transportation would allow, they were in London by early June, where they sought out Coleridge before they could sail home.

Channing presented the Sage of Highgate with letters of introduction from Allston, and the two spent some time discussing him. The Coleridge whom Channing visited was very different from the young revolutionary who had shouted over the successes of the French Revolution. He had not only stopped worrying about political movements but also explicitly rejected his old religious heresies. The Unitarianism of his youth had long since evaporated, and his devotion to Hartley and Priestley had given way to an evangelical type of piety. He now believed there could be no morality without religion and no religion without revelation.[61] Christianity was for him, as it was for Channing, "the only Revelation of permanent and universal validity."[62] "He was so delighted," Channing said later, "to get a patient ear for his cherished thoughts, that he poured them out in a flood on all subjects,—the transcendental philosophy, Trinitarianism and Unitarianism, and especially on his idea of the Church of England, which was wholly new to me for he included all the spiritual forces at work in the land—the great schools and universities, and even the sectarian schools and pulpits."[63]

In comparison with Coleridge, most of the English people whom Channing afterwards met seemed rather lackadaisical. This was not true, however, of Lucy Aikin, the niece of the celebrated English moralist and critic Anna Barbauld. Although their meeting was somewhat by chance, Channing and Miss Aikin began a discussion that was continued by letters for more than sixteen years. She became to Channing a lifelong confidante and, in one sense, a kind of safety valve. Through her he was also able to keep abreast of developments in England and on the Continent, neither of which he was ever to see again after sailing for home late in the summer of 1823.

Channing's European travels were highly significant both for him and for the cultural liberation of those whom he was to influence. Several years earlier he had been pleased to note that certain writers of Wordsworth's school had made the discovery "that Unitarianism and imagination and poetry are not irreconcilable foes."[64] And later he wrote: "I smile when I hear poetry called light reading. The true poet has far-reaching thoughts, a perception of the harmonious and exquisite relations of the universe, an eye that pierces the depths and the miseries of the soul, placing him amidst the most gifted and exalted intelligences."[65] His cultural horizon had begun to open, therefore, even before his trip abroad. Unlike many of the liberals, he was not content merely to consolidate the material gains resulting from victory over the orthodox. He knew that the theological break had come but that the cultural still waited to be realized. He knew, also, that the Calvinism of the early "Saints" and the "New Light" doctrines of Jonathan Edwards had possessed power to arouse emotions and kindle imagination that was seriously lacking in current Unitarianism.

Temperamentally opposed to the negations of Unitarianism and firmly convinced of the possibilities of human nature, Channing realized fully the danger of the liberalism's degenerating into another orthodoxy. So he turned to the English romantics for the development of imagination and poetical enthusiasm to supplement the "partial culture of the mind" afforded by the empirical philosophy and sensational psychology of his day. His visits with Wordsworth, Southey, and Coleridge and his experience of the natural surroundings and cultural environment of the Old World confirmed opinions previously formed through reading. As a result, a warmer current of life had been breathed into his cold New England theology. Boston was still in its month of March; Channing had been touched by the springs of romanticism. Henceforth, they would invigorate the entire stream of his ideas about philosophy and social reforms.

Although his European trip had inspired him spiritually, it had done little for him physically. He again asked his church for help, and arrangements were made for a full-time assistant. In the fall of 1823, Ezra Stiles Gannett became the colleague at Federal Street who relieved him of many pressing duties. For the first time in many years Channing was able to devote time to interests not strictly pastoral. Preaching was still, however, the work into which he poured his entire being— as young Waldo Emerson could attest. No longer one of Channing's parishioners, Emerson walked into Boston from Roxbury almost every Sunday to hear him preach. Granting even that Channing cherished certain beliefs—such as Christ's pre-existence, the historicity of scripture, and miracles, which Emerson no longer held—Waldo still found him closer to his own way of thinking than any other minister around. Later he would take a "hebdomadal walk" to Dr. Channing "for the sake of saying I am studying divinity."[66]

VII *Publications—and Abolition*

Most Bostonians would have accepted in the mid-1820's an assessment of Dr. Channing as an eloquent minister whose words in the pulpit were matched by his actions in society, sometimes to the discomfiture of even the more enlightened members of the community. But many were at first surprised and later overly enthusiastic when his essay "Remarks on the Character of John Milton" appeared in the *Christian Examiner* (the old *Disciple* under a new name and editorial policy) in 1826. During the next four years, most of the essays upon which his international reputation as a leading American author depended were written. The two parts of the "Remarks on the Character and Writings of Fénelon" graced the pages of the *Examiner* the following year, as did his article "The Union." And in his "Remarks on National Literature" of 1830 he anticipated Emerson's "The American Scholar." The same year he collected and revised the most representative of his past efforts for publication under the title of *Discourses, Reviews, and Miscellanies.* Two years later he published a second volume of sermons in order to earn money he had pledged to the Boston Farm School.

One of the sermons included in the 1830 volume of *Discourses* was his "Likeness to God," preached at the ordination of Frederick A. Farley in 1828. This—the most effective statement of transcendentalism he was ever to make—and "Spiritual Freedom," his address to the State Senate in 1830, were his last great affronts to New England orthodoxy. By the same token they represented how far he had traveled from the Calvinism and Federalism of his youth. And if the truth were told, his travels had taken him beyond the sympathies of many of his parishioners who preferred their Christianity in the abstract and their minister in the clouds—far removed from public affairs!

In the spring of 1826 Sarah Hale, author of "Mary Had a Little Lamb," wrote Congressman Edward Everett that "Parson Channing" was "half mad on the subject of slavery."[67] But it wasn't until the fall of 1830 that Channing was to learn some lessons firsthand from a "volume of slavery opened always before [his] eyes."[68] He had taken his wife to St. Croix in the West Indies so that they both could have a rest cure. The island air was salubrious; but, as he wrote Andrews Norton, he found slavery "the most interesting object in the state of society . . . though I see it in one of its mildest forms, I look on it with increasing aversion."[69] Later he wrote Norton that the era was one of change: revolution was in progress, and religion and politics would have to advance or be left behind.[70] His response to the new spirit reflected his faith that the future would bring great improvements.

Upon his return to Boston, Channing preached a sermon about the evils of slavery with particular emphasis on the moral harm to mind and soul. From this time on, the affection of many members of his congregation began to cool. The proximate cause of their hypersensitivity was not Channing himself but a much more outspoken advocate of freedom for the Negroes: William Lloyd Garrison, who in January, 1831, had started his *Liberator* in Boston. "I will be heard" had been his battle cry, and Bostonians were beginning to learn that he had not been idly boasting. Many of them, however, were like Elizabeth Peabody; they thought Garrison's editorials "the most unchristian and unreasonable violence and indiscriminate rage against the whole South, and most of the North as well."[71]

Channing at once became a subscriber to Garrison's paper. He agreed with Garrison's main principle that it was wrong to make a chattel of a human being, but he doubted Garrison's ideas. He was unable to look upon slaveholders in the mass as Garrison did. To him they were individuals and their guilt could not be measured collectively.

Unhappily, the first effects of abolition led Channing to defer participation in the growing opposition to slavery. While still at Saint Croix, he had already begun to write an essay which he thought of addressing to the South as an open letter. But when he returned to find Garrison agitating for immediate action, he decided to wait. The most unfavorable construction of his motives came from his own parishioner Maria Chapman. "He had neither insight, courage nor firmness," she wrote in her appendix to the autobiography of Harriet Martineau. "He had been selected by a set of money-making men as their

representative for piety, as Edward Everett was their representative gentleman and scholar, Judge Story their representative jurist and companion in social life, and Daniel
Webster their representative statesman and advocate looking
after their interests in Congress."[72] But nothing could have
been farther from the truth as her friend Harriet Martineau
affirmed: "He has shown what his moral courage is by proofs
which will long outlast his indications of slowness in admitting
the full merits of the Abolitionists."[73]

Soon after Channing's St. Croix visit, Samuel May—"the
Lord's chore boy," as Bronson Alcott labeled him—began to
meet with Channing to talk about the abolitionist cause. At
one of these meetings in the autumn of 1834, May forgot his
usual deference and began to debate with Channing about
Abolitionism. "His principal, if not his only objections," May
declared, "were alleged against the severity of our denunci-
ations, the harshness of our language, the vehemence, the
heat, and excitement caused by our meetings."[74]

Channing continued his objections until May broke out
warmly: "Dr. Channing, I am tired of these complaints . . . it
is not our fault, that those who might have managed this
reform more prudently have left us to manage it as we may be
able. It is not our fault that those who might have pleaded
for the enslaved so much more eloquently, both with the pen
and with the living voice, than we can, have been silent. We
are not to blame, sir, that you, who, perhaps more than any
other man, might have so raised the voice of remonstrance that
it should have been heard throughout the length and breadth
of the land,—we are not to blame, sir, that you have not
spoken. And now because inferior men have begun to speak
and act against what you yourself acknowledge to be an
awful injustice, it is not becoming in you to complain to us,
because we do it in an inferior style. Why, sir, have you not
moved, why have you not spoken before?"[75] When Channing's
reply came, it was uttered in a low but steady voice: "Brother
May, I acknowledge the justice of your reproof; I have been
silent too long."[76]

From this time on, Channing was consistently vocal against
slavery. Only a few weeks after the mobbing of Garrison on
Boston Commons in October, 1835, the publication of Chan-

ning's pamphlet on "Slavery" identified him squarely with the antislavery cause. Although some of the Abolitionists were critical because he did not go far enough in his condemnation of slaveholders but went too far in his censure of Abolitionists' excesses, John Quincy Adams declared the pamphlet to be "in fact an inflammatory if not incendiary publication."[77] Certainly Channing's own people at Federal Street were so incensed they cut him on the street.

But as Channing told Elizabeth Peabody, "I care little for opinion, because it does not run in my channel."[78] From this time on until his death, much of his energy was spent in thinking, writing, and talking about slavery without regard for the way the winds of opinion might blow; but he continued to exercise his usual caution in deferring action until he was as certain as he could be of the grounds on which he was proceeding. In 1836 he published an open letter to James G. Birney, an Ohio antislavery editor, defending the right of Abolitionists to speak freely against slavery. The following summer, he completed an open letter to Henry Clay entitled "On the Annexation of Texas," which is, of all his contributions to antislavery, the most cogent and best adapted to its end.

When news reached Boston of the murder of Elizah Lovejoy, who died defending his antislavery press in Alton, Illinois, Channing was largely responsible for the protest meeting that drew nearly five thousand spectators to Faneuil Hall on December 8. Channing not only addressed the crowd but listened while his prepared resolutions concerning freedom of speech and press were read. The meeting promised to end uneventfully until Attorney General James T. Austin jumped to his feet to denounce Channing's resolutions as "abstract propositions," to declare that Lovejoy had "died as the fool dieth," and to liken the mob of Alton to the fathers of the American Revolution. His remarks met with a tremendous roar from the crowd, and it appeared for the moment that he might turn sentiment against the resolutions. But Jonathan Phillips, the chairman, turned to Channing and said, "Can you stand thunder?" Channing replied, "Such thunder as this, in any measure."[79] Then young Wendell Phillips strode to the platform and silenced the hecklers. When Phillips' last

word was uttered, bedlam broke loose. His bravery and eloquence had turned the tide of sentiment, and Channing's
resolutions were passed.

Channing's participation in the Faneuil Hall meeting was
further cause for more of his parishioners and friends to fall
away. But while his actions had identified him with the
Abolitionists, a letter from him to *The Liberator,* within a
week of his appearance at Faneuil Hall, did much to offset
gains among the Abolitionists themselves. In that letter, he
called upon them to disavow the appeal to force. Garrison's
reaction was immediate. He called Channing's letter "defec-
tive in principle, false in its charity, and inconsistent in its
reasoning."[80]

As a man of action who was temperamentally inclined to
move in a direct line to his objectives, Garrison could not
understand Channing's inveterate, cautious delay of action
until he was reasonably certain of the moral rightness of his
decisions. The two were a study in contrast; and, since public
opinion so often decides against the more conservative approach to human problems, it is little wonder that Channing's
contemporaries sometimes thought him timid and lacking in
courage. Yet Channing's habitual dependence upon reason
and careful investigation did not indicate a lack of courage
certainly, for he entered frays from which many a stronger
man shrank; and once he had determined the rightness of
an act, he never counted the cost. Certainly a mere pragmatist
would not have intervened to free Abner Kneeland from a
prison sentence for having "wilfully denied the existence of
God," but Channing did because he believed even atheists
were entitled to express their views.

The accusation that he was a "white-handed reformer"
having little or no knowledge of practical realities fails to
account for Channing's usually being in advance of his contemporaries in social reform. Though he idealized overmuch—
and he was even capable of idealizing the efforts of the poor
to improve their own lot—his lectures on "Self-Culture" in
1838 and "On the Elevation of the Laboring Classes" in 1840
show that he had gained considerable insight into the material
causes of human misery since his experiences at Harvard and
in Virginia.

The subject of the expansiveness of the age that lay ahead comprised the greater share of his address to the Mercantile Library Company in Philadelphia in the spring of 1841. He foresaw great developments by mid-century, and he conceded that they might involve drastic change and even social upheaval. But he declared: "The mass must not be confined and kept down through a vague dread of revolutions. A social order requiring such a sacrifice would be too dearly bought."[81] Reforms were needed in every sphere, he acknowledged, but the impulse to change was growing stronger everywhere. It was the duty of right-thinking men, therefore, to remove the roadblocks that lay athwart progress.

For his own part, Channing chose to spend his last years concentrating on the evil of slavery. Every word he uttered about this subject was now cause for further estrangement of his parishioners. The crowning hurt was given when the church officers of Federal Street refused to honor his request that the church be used for a memorial service for Charles Follen, a cherished friend and fellow-worker in the anti-slavery cause. Follen, a German refugee from persecution abroad, had long been close to Channing; and his tragic death by fire during a boat trip from New York to Boston had left Channing sad and somewhat depressed. The refusal of his own society led him for a time to question whether his ministry had any usefulness at all.

But he did not despair. In the latter part of 1840 he started Elizabeth Peabody on her publishing career with his manuscript *Emancipation*. Two years later, he published, after careful research, a double pamphlet in which he took issue with Daniel Webster about the *Creole* case, an international legal tangle arising out of the mutiny by Negro slaves aboard the brig *Creole*. His final public address was delivered on August 1, 1842, at Lenox, Massachusetts, in the beautiful valley of the Housatonic. Since it was the anniversary of West Indian Emancipation, Channing chose the occasion to hold England's example up to his countrymen as an object lesson. Showing his complete disdain for slaveholders who appealed to fear to justify their position, he stated forthrightly, "The question of slavery is a question of property. . . . The master holds fast his slave because he sees in him, not a wild beast, but a profitable chattel."[82] For the North to have any part in such dealing would be entirely wrong: "First we must free ourselves . . . from all constitutional or legal obligations to uphold slavery."[83] In the next place, "the North has one weapon,—moral force" to fight with.[84] This alone would not suffice, but it had to be used if the other factors that were to bring about the end of slavery were to have their full effect.

Channing spoke eloquently and powerfully to his Lenox audience; but, when the address was over, he was completely spent. After several weeks of rest, he began his return journey to Boston; but an attack of typhoid fever forced him to bed in Bennington, Vermont. His family was called to his side and there, in sight of the mountains he cherished and in the midst of his loved ones, he died on October 2, 1842. His body was taken to Boston, and on October 7, funeral services were held in the Federal Street Church. Interment was in Mount Auburn Cemetery.

There were countless testimonies to Channing's greatness both in America and abroad, but none was more sincere or moving than the "humble tribute" of Theodore Parker. "I hesitate not to say," declared Parker, "that since Washington, no man has died amongst us whose real influence was so wide. and so beneficent, both abroad and at home. . . . He did not see all the truth that will be seen in the next century. He did what was better, he helped men to see somewhat of truth in this, and blessed all that aided others to see."[85]

CHAPTER 2

Religious and Ethical Views

WHEN William Ellery Channing was consecrated to the ministry in the Federal Street Church of Boston in June, 1803, he embarked on an intellectual voyage that set him apart eventually not only from his New England contemporaries but also from his fellows in religion everywhere. Although an illustrious career lay ahead of him, the state of religion in and around Boston at the time of his settlement provided clues to a future period of controversy as well as reminders that the course of the New England minister had seldom been straight or easy throughout the entire history of religion from Puritan times down to the post-Revolutionary era.

For Channing the road of religious orthodoxy would soon lose its attractiveness, although it was well traveled by men of good faith and intelligence and had been identified in his mind from boyhood as the tried-and-true way to God and salvation. But the path of dissent—though he had made only the most tentative exploration of it and hence could understand but dimly the full implications of what he saw—was also clearly marked out by the time he began to take his place in the Boston firmament.

In 1805—with the appointment of Henry Ware as Hollis Professor of Divinity at Harvard to fill the vacancy left by the death of David Tappan, Channing's former teacher and mentor in religious studies—dissent developed into an open controversy that affected New Englanders as deeply as the Great Awakening had seventy years before. By the time it was finished more than thirty years later, Channing would stand forth as the acknowledged leader of the Unitarians, a group identified by their orthodox opponents as hardly Christian. More clearly viewed from the perspective of the present day, they are seen as builders upon the inheritance accumulated for them by two generations of religious dissenters whose characteristic doctrines began to emerge at the time of the Great Awakening in the 1740's. These were the Arminians, who counted among their number some of the most distinguished minds in New England; and they form a long line from Charles Chauncy, Edwards' opponent in the Awakening, through Ebenezer Gay, Lemuel Briant, and Jonathan Mayhew to Joseph Stevens Buckminster and Channing himself.[1] Before any account of Channing's particular role in New England ecclesiastical history can be given, it becomes necessary, therefore, to retrace, if only briefly, the course of religious liberalism in the century preceding his ministry.

I *The Beginnings of Unitarianism*

Even before the ground swell of revivalism reached New England and Jonathan Edwards in Northampton in 1735, there were numerous indications that a softening process had been going on within New England Calvinism almost from the very inception of the Puritan theocracy. As soon as the early settlers had found a breathing spell from their labors and after they had proved themselves equal to the demands of life in a wilderness, they began to develop a spirit of independence in spite of their belief in a supreme being whose will was law. Puritanism was inherently individualistic because its covenant theology made salvation a private matter between man and his God; furthermore, the conditions of colonial life were exactly those most likely to develop this individualism into a full-blown self-reliance.[2]

The process of emancipation from the Calvinistic tenets of total depravity, predestination, and election had started early—as soon, in fact, as the fervor of the first generation of Puritan "saints" failed to renew itself in their children and, to a much greater extent, in their children's children. Despite measures like the halfway covenant to stem the growing tide of the unchurched, the seventeenth century closed with increasing signs of indifference to major Puritan beliefs. The theocracy—a comprehensive theological system designed to integrate ethics, politics, economics, science, and social matters —was beginning to weaken. In the early eighteenth century, the forces of a new *Zeitgeist* brought additional pressure to bear, and the theocracy began to crumble from within.

But a new champion was found in Jonathan Edwards, whose early conversion to Calvinism led him to defend it against all unbelievers in terms that made sense to eighteenth-century minds. To Edwards, one of the chief enemies of Calvinism was Arminianism, a generic term used broadly to characterize any effort to emphasize human initiative at the expense of divine sovereignty. Anyone who denied that God elects man for salvation regardless of his moral worth and who claimed that man's behavior as a free agent determines whether he is saved was an Arminian. Whether they knew it or not, claimed Edwards, many of his parishioners and fellow citizens had been seduced by heresy from abroad (many Anglican churchmen were known to be Arminians) and were actually mouthing only words when they professed belief in the faith of their grandfathers. Indeed, they were acting just as though their wills were self-determining and needed only a little coaxing to choose goodness.[3]

Edwards' efforts on behalf of an undiluted Calvinism never flagged; but, when the revivalistic practices of itinerant preachers like George Whitefield, Gilbert Tennent, and John Davenport proved efficacious, Edwards, reared in the evangelical atmosphere of the Connecticut valley, eagerly accepted the revival as a working of the spirit of God although he deplored the excesses of a lunatic fringe who delighted in arousing emotions to a frenzy. Not so Charles Chauncy, a Harvard graduate and junior minister at the First Church in Boston, who not only frowned on all forms of enthusiasm but also spearheaded the opposition in Boston and its vicinity to Edwards and the revival.[4]

The Great Awakening—as the series of revivals between 1735 and 1745 have come to be known—was a complex religious and social phenomenon that used the language of theological controversy to cloak deep-seated economic, political, and social unrest. In general, the majority of Harvard-trained ministers, who served churches in Massachusetts and

Connecticut as far west as the Connecticut river, opposed the revival; but Yale graduates, concentrated for the most part in the Connecticut Valley, favored it. Certainly the debate between Edwards and Chauncy indicates a division along these lines although temperamental and intellectual differences also set them widely apart.

Both Chauncy and Edwards distrusted enthusiasm, but they differed in their judgment of human emotion. As a sober and somewhat unimaginative rationalist, Chauncy believed the emotions had to be kept subject to the will and thus to reason. Since the revival seemed to him to by-pass reason, he opposed it. On the other hand, Edwards, holding that the emotions were synonymous with the will and neither good nor bad in themselves, could and did make use of them in his work of bringing souls to God.[5] How effective his method could be is shown by the success of his "Sinners in the Hands of An Angry God" (1741), which was delivered without any of the shownmanship or spellbinding techniques of ranters like Davenport or roarers like Whitefield.

By 1745, when the pent-up energy that had made the Great Awakening possible was expended, the unity of the Congregational Church was shattered; and a cleavage was established which would result eventually in a Unitarian denomination. Within the Congregational family there were now two factions: on one side stood the Calvinists, themselves divided into New Lights and Old Lights; on the other were the Rationalists, who had little thought when they became the party of the opposition that they were starting down the path to Arminianism. The Old Lights, rejecting the progressive psychology of Edwards, were still fighting the Enlightenment in a vain attempt to keep the doctrine of the Puritan "saints" alive. The New Lights, led by Edwards, who had learned from Newton and Locke the value of the New Science and the New Philosophy, were prepared to defend their ideas with a religious psychology that was well ahead of its time.

After the furor of revivalism had passed, New England thinkers awakened to the fact that the Enlightenment was in their midst. Reason had been enthroned in England and on the continent for some time; now a number of its streams of influence were beginning to pour into the whole of New

England, where hitherto they had only seeped, by one devious way or another, into certain isolated spots. Several of these influences were important in shaping the future of Arminianism.

For one thing, rationalists like Chauncy and Jonathan Mayhew began to apply the test of reason to scriptural analysis. By collecting and comparing texts and using techniques of linguistic study developed by English dissenters, they laid the foundation for the type of theological training received by Unitarians in the following century.[6] Although by no means the kind of exegesis developed later by scientific German scholarship, it did employ reason to an extent that the orthodox were unwilling to accept.

By the 1750's the Arminians began to use the rationalist position to attack openly the doctrine of original sin preached by the Calvinists. Since guilt to the Arminians was a personal matter, the individual could not be held responsible for the sins of his father—even if the parent were Father Adam himself. They admitted that man contained a mixture of good and evil and that human passions had to be controlled, but they argued that God had given him reason and an inborn moral sense called conscience to guide him and provide a balance against his appetites.

This more reasonable approach to human nature led naturally to a different view of the Divine Nature. In 1751 John Bass couched the moral argument against depravity in practically the same language that Channing used seventy years later:

> . . . representing our Nature as exceeding Corrupt and Wicked as soon as formed, odious to God's Holiness and under his Wrathe and Curse; has, so far as I can see a natural Tendency to fill the Mind with the most gloomy Apprehensions of the Author of our Being, to damp our Spirits, to turn away our Hearts from Him; and, in a Word, to the Destruction of all Religion.[7]

Like most of his colleagues, however, Bass considered human nature frail and prone to sin; the time was still not ripe for a full affirmation of human dignity and worth.

Closely related to the problem of whether man is corrupt

was the question of his freedom as a moral agent. Jonathan Edwards' *Freedom of the Will* (1754) established a doctrine of moral necessity, but his Arminian opponents against whom it was directed could not be convinced. Since they believed in general that human nature was determined by environmental influences, they rejected completely the idea of man's inheritance of Adam's guilt. Actually, Edwards was far more concerned about the problem of will than the Arminians. Experience led them to believe that they were free to determine their acts, and most of all free of any inherited restriction upon their reason or conscience.

The positive side of the Arminians' denial of election and original sin was contained in their doctrine of justification and regeneration. Although they never argued for a justification by works or personal righteousness, they reinterpreted the Puritan covenant between God and man to mean that all men—not just the elect—had an equal opportunity to accept or reject the terms by which God would save those who believed in him and who sought to do his will. A man's faith then was a condition for salvation, but it was manifest by earnest desire and good deeds. In all but words the Arminian position eliminated the distinction between grace and works.

Over the subject of regeneration a triangular dispute arose. The Old Calvinists were forced into siding first with the New Lights and then with the Arminians. All three parties agreed that man could do nothing by himself, but grace meant something different to each of them. To the Arminians, it was nothing special, since they had discarded the idea of election. But the Old and New Lights still clung to a covenant of grace. For New Light leader Samuel Hopkins, regeneration was an instantaneous act by which God came into a man's heart. With this interpretation the Old Lights were agreed, but they also emphasized the gradual development of the moral powers after regeneration. Only the gradual development, or conversion, was stressed by the Arminians. Men like Mayhew believed that justification was a standard toward which man must continually strive, and they stressed the fact that man's spiritual powers were capable of development from birth onward. For Mayhew and many others like him, the substance of Christian duty consisted in the love of God and one's neighbor and in the practice of morality rather than in mere belief in any creed.[8]

At the same time that the Arminians defended man's ability to do God's will, they also maintained his ability to know what it was. The Puritans had believed that man's reason was darkened and made unworthy of reliance through Adam's fall; consequently, the will of God could be known only through special revelations incorporated in the Scriptures: Holy Writ was to be accepted by faith, yet no violence was to be done to reason. But to the Arminians the supernatural rationalism stemming from Newtonian physics and Lockean psychology provided a rich source for the new rationalism and a shift in emphasis became noticeable. More and more the test of reason began to be applied to revelation, private as well as scriptural.

Reason, according to English uniformitarians, was the same in all men; but Chauncy and Mayhew argued that mental powers differed. "Our intellectual faculties," said Mayhew, "were given us to improve: they rust for want of use; but are brightened by exercise."[9] The capacity for growth and enlargement he suggested was later extended to man's moral and social development. "It is in consequence of this capacity," Chauncy declared, "that we suppose . . . that all intelligent moral beings, in all worlds, are continually going on, while they suitably employ and improve their original faculties, from one degree of attainment to another; and, hereupon, from one degree of happiness to another, without end."[10]

From Chauncy's time on, reason became so closely identified with religion that it was difficult to distinguish them. Natural religion, or "that which unassisted reason can discover and prove," contained three essentials: the existence of God, the obligations of piety to God and benevolence to men, and a doctrine of future rewards and punishments. It was still to be differentiated from revealed religion, but the distinction between the two was gradually so blurred that the Dudleian lecturer in 1779, Gad Hitchcock, could say to Harvard undergraduates: "Natural religion is not so properly defined to be that, which mankind have, or might come to the knowledge of, merely by the strength of unassisted reason; as that, which reason sees to be right, and feels the force of, when it is known."[11]

As the theological sanctions of the previous century began to dissolve, the eighteenth century became preoccupied with the obligations of piety and benevolence. English rationalists like John Locke and Samuel Clarke favored an intellectual ethic. Since God always acts in accordance with the eternal fitness of things, they said, rational creatures should do likewise. Humanitarians like Shaftesbury and Hutcheson, believing in an inborn moral sense, claimed that man chooses good not for reward but because it is naturally agreeable. Joseph Butler went a step further when he insisted that conscience drives men to *do* good, not merely to *approve* it. In New England, Mayhew and Chauncy accepted both Clarke and Hutcheson while Chauncy borrowed from Butler as well. At mid-century Hutcheson was prescribed at Harvard.[12]

From the time of the Puritans and even until the American Revolution, most men had pictured God as a king and father and his government as a constitutional monarchy. But the Calvinists' insistence that God acted only for his own glory was opposed by the Arminians, who were adamant in their stand that man's happiness was the end for which God worked. As the idea of monarchy came into disrepute in politics, it also began to lose its force in liberal theology. In its place the concept of the fatherhood of God and his moral government began to gain credence; and, of course, this change in attitude created new problems for the liberals. Could a truly benevolent Deity condemn any of his creatures to destruction? Some of the Arminian apologists offered lame excuses, but Chauncy attacked the problem more directly in a work called *The Salvation of All Men: the Grand Thing Aimed at in the Scheme of God.*[13] No man, said Chauncy, will be condemned eternally because God's plans call for him to attain ultimately to virtue after enduring a trial and discipline that will continue into life after death.

Universalism, as Chauncy's solution was called, attracted many adherents; but it still did not explain how one might reconcile the goodness of God with the existence of moral and physical evil. Various solutions were given, but none were satisfactory. When all was said and resaid, the Arminians had to admit that God permitted evil. Life was a time of trial, and man's fitness for eternal happiness was determined by the manner in which he disciplined himself to encounter life's problems.

Although there was no necessary connection between Arminianism and disbelief in the doctrine of the Trinity, the orthodox commonly assumed, and not without reason, that most Arminians were at least Arians, if not Socinians, in their Christology. Anti-Trinitarianism had existed for a long time in New England, but it was not until mid-eighteenth century that Mayhew in his *Seven Sermons* (1755) openly attacked the Athanasian doctrine. He was probably responsible also for republishing the next year that standard edition of English Arianism, Thomas Emlyn's *Inquiry*.[14] Mayhew turned his attention to political matters after these two efforts; but Simeon Howard, his successor at the West Church in Boston, was attacked for doctrinal unsoundness by Samuel Hopkins, who preached a strongly worded Trinitarian sermon in Boston because he was convinced that "the doctrine of the Divinity of Christ was much neglected, if not disbelieved by a number of the ministers of Boston."[15] If anything, Hopkins was guilty of understatement.

For the most part, the first generation of Arminians were Arians, who believed, as did Englishmen like Samuel Clarke and Thomas Emlyn, that Christ was a pre-existent being inferior to God the Father but more than mere man. Few of them indeed were willing to advocate openly, as did representatives of a later generation like James Freeman of King's Chapel and William Bentley of the East Church in Salem, the doctrines of English Socinians like Joseph Priestley and the elder William Hazlitt. The latter believed Christ to be simply human but unique in his providential mission as the greatest of the sons of God.[16]

Christ's function as mediator between God and man made most of the liberals hesitate about Socinianism; and their emphasis on divine benevolence was as much responsible as their anti-Trinitarianism for their reassessment of the doctrine of atonement. According to the Anselmic theory—which carried the imprimatur of Roman Catholicism and which had been adopted by Calvinism and later reasserted by Jonathan Edwards with his own peculiar emphasis—since God had been infinitely offended by the sin of Adam and Eve, the only possible redeemer was another infinite being, Christ the God-man. The relationship was similar to that of creditor and debtor.

In the eighteenth century, however, justice was defined as the enforcement of just laws designed to establish order rather than the punishment of transgressions. The governmental theory of atonement, derived from Hugo Grotius, the great Renaissance jurist, seemed more in keeping with the spirit of the age. According to Grotius, God was a Ruler who must maintain order and prevent crime. He must insist on obedience, but He might remit penalties to wrongdoers when He saw fit. Christ's death was, then, not a ransom for sinners but merely an example to them and a warning of the horrible nature and consequences of sin. This theory was adopted by most of the Arminians because it enabled them to emphasize the benevolence of God and reject the idea that Christ was its cause. Bit by bit, however, they abandoned even the Grotian concept. In place of the traditional doctrine that Christ was a king, who judged transgression; a priest, who interceded for man before the throne of the Father; and a prophet, who was the chief source of revelation of God's will, they substituted the idea that Christ's unparalleled virtue provided men with inspiration for their own lives.

During all the time that the text of New England theology was being revised by the liberals, the orthodox had, of course, resisted every change with all the force they commanded. At first, every effort was made to hold Congregationalism together. But as tempers warmed and the breach widened, orthodox believers began to smoke out dissenters. As early as the 1750's, according to John Adams, Church covenants began to be revised to include doctrinal standards for admission.[17] The Arminians denounced this "system of exclusion" and persistently fought the use of creeds and confessions of faith as tests of orthodoxy. Since they took for granted differences of interpretation resulting from the study of the Scriptures, they did not believe in any society's imposition of creeds. Private judgment, as they saw it, was not only a right but a duty. Diversity of opinion, far from being an evil, became a necessity for any institution that hoped to grow and improve. However eloquently the Arminians defended spiritual freedom, the record shows that the orthodox intensified their efforts at excluding them from church fellowship; and as the century drew to a close, feeling was beginning to run high in a great many congregations.

There was one issue, however, about which the orthodox and Arminians stood as one: the subject of infidelity. Deism had hung on the outskirts of rationalism throughout the entire eighteenth century, but it wasn't until after the Revolution that it was considered a serious threat to revealed religion. Tension mounted in the eighties, but the appearance of Tom Paine's *Age of Reason* in 1794 caused open alarm.[18] Both Arminians and Calvinists condemned Paine, but students at Harvard and Yale, as we have seen,[19] were so attracted that the college authorities were concerned lest irreligion take over.

In essence, the threat of deism to religion was its two-pronged attack on the institutional aspects of Christianity and on the evidences of its divine origin and authority—revelation and the miracles of Christ. Although in many ways the deists were very close to the supernatural rationalists of the Enlightenment in their use of rational inquiry, they differed from them, especially after the time of Locke, in their organized opposition to everything but the lowest common denominator in religion, which amounted for men like Paine and Ethan Allen to little more than morality and a belief in a deity who was human reason writ large. For less extreme deists like Jefferson, Franklin, and Madison, church membership and a more orthodox branch of Christianity still remained possible. But in general, deists believed in a personal rather than an institutional religion, in reason rather than faith, and in science and nature rather than the Bible.[20]

The actual extent of the influence of deism in America is difficult to measure both because of exaggerated claims of the deists themselves and because of the exaggeration of their power by the ministers who fought them. A typical example of the latter is the claim made by Jedidiah Morse in a fast-day sermon, preached during Channing's senior year at Harvard, that the deists were behind an international conspiracy to overthrow church and state in America just as they had been responsible for the revolution in France and the reign of terror that followed.[21] Morse was never able to prove his case; but, staunchly orthodox as he was and an ardent Federalist, he provides proof of another factor about infidelity that should be remarked. Throughout the century, the growing secularism and the increase of democracy had tended to undermine the prestige of the whole class of ministers, a group whose position in the Puritan theocracy was almost comparable to that of titled nobility under a monarchy. The shift from religion to politics had been gradual, but the balance of prestige was plainly with the lawyer and politician by the century's end. Thus, as Morse clearly saw, the defense of religion was the defense of Federalism; and opposition to republicans like Jefferson and Paine meant opposition to infidelity and French egalitarianism.

Before the Revolution, none were more patriotic than the liberal New England ministers in defending the colonial cause; during the thirty years that followed independence, none were more staunch than these same ministers in supporting liberal religions as well as Washington and Adams and the federalistic cause. Many examples could be cited to prove this point, but none would be so appropriate as that of the Reverend William Ellery Channing, Federalist son of a Federalist father, Christian rationalist, and heir to the Arminian legacy of liberal religion.

II   *The Inheritance of the Enlightenment*

Although Channing joined the Adelphi (a club for students intending to become ministers) when he was a junior at Harvard, it was not until the end of his senior year that he became actively interested in the ministry. As he himself stated, "the prevalence of infidelity imported from France led me to inquire into the evidences of Christianity, and then *I found for what I was made*."[22] The following October he was writing his former classmate William Shaw: "Yes, Shaw, I shall be a minister, . . . a reformer of a vicious, and an instructor of an ignorant world. . . . In my view, religion is but another name for happiness, and I am most cheerful when I am most religious."[23]

In a very real sense, then, Channing's decision to become a minister was based upon sentiments characteristic of a man of the Enlightenment. The emphasis upon rational enquiry and the finding of evidence to support religious belief; the possibility of reform through increase of knowledge; and religion as "the pursuit of happiness"—these are hallmarks of the rational Christianity that developed during the eighteenth century and gave impetus in the early nineteenth century to what has been called the Second Great Awakening of American Protestantism. But any attempt to account for the unique influence exerted by Channing during that Awakening must consider first of all how his eclectic system of religion and philosophy was welded together.

As Channing's own reference to French infidelity indicates and as the beginnings of Unitarianism clearly prove, thoughtful minds in post-Revolutionary America experienced a strong need for a philosophy that could be used to bolster religion against its enemies. In the colleges in particular the need arose from a concrete situation of growing skepticism and irreligion.[24] The presentation by the Corporation at Harvard of a copy of Bishop Watson's *Apology for the Bible* to each student as an antidote to Paine's *Age of Reason* is representative of the apologetical spirit that quickly developed in Harvard, Princeton, and Yale. But secular rationalism was gnawing away at the whole fabric of the New England Calvinistic theology, and the admirable work of Jonathan Edwards and his followers to keep it intact was no longer fruitful. More effective means than the good bishop's *Apology* were needed; and the answer was found in the doctrines of the Scotch moderates, the philosophers of Common Sense, whose system lent itself readily to exposition in essay form, sermons, and public lectures.

During Channing's tenure at Harvard the Scottish philosophy was introduced into the curriculum by a moderate Calvinist, David Tappan, the Hollis Professor of Divinity. If not directly, it was at least under his general influence that Channing read first Thomas Reid's treatise on the human mind

(1764) and later Francis Hutcheson. Tappan himself was a believer in disinterested benevolence, but it was Hutcheson's *Inquiry* (1725) that first brought home to Channing the full realization of what the doctrine meant. Hutcheson's concept of a moral sense that was as much a part of man as his leg or arm and that enabled him to perceive morality as he saw a physical object and to direct his actions unselfishly to the good of others seemed to Channing to give proper value for the first time to human dignity.[25]

Despite this feeling, he could not insulate himself completely from the influence of Locke, whose *Essay on Human Understanding* had been used as a textbook at Harvard for more than a half century before Channing's arrival. But Lockean empiricism was becoming increasingly unsatisfactory to many people of the late eighteenth century, and Channing himself testified that Richard Price provided him with an answer to Locke's philosophy. "He gave me the doctrine of ideas, and during my life I have written the words Love, Right, etc., with a capital. That book probably moulded my philosophy into the form it has always retained."[26]

The book in question was Price's *Morals* (1769), which Channing read during his junior and senior years in college. In the *Morals* Price had attempted to refute both the skepticism of Hume toward matters of factual knowledge and Hutcheson's concept of a moral sense. Unlike Hutcheson, who made morality a matter of the successful operation or failure of the moral *sense* and thus seemingly eliminated choice by a moral *agent*, Price believed that man possessed a power of *understanding* to determine right from wrong. In what almost approached the distinction that Kant was to draw between the theoretical and practical reason, Price argued that the understanding is different from the reason which "consists in investigating certain relations between objects, ideas of which must have been previously in the mind: that is, it supposes us already to have the ideas we want to trace; and therefore cannot give rise to new ideas."[27] He went on to conclude: "It is undeniable that many of our ideas are derived from the INTUITION of the truth, or the discernment of the natures of things by the understanding of our moral ideas."[28]

In Price's idealistic philosophy, pleasure and pain are not to be confused with virtue and vice; they are merely effects or concomitants. Moreover, "Virtue and vice . . . from the *natures of things,* are the most constant and intimate causes of private happiness and misery."[29] The recognition of this fact rather than utility or the lack of it is the source of virtue. And those who assume that the will of God is antecedent to the "universal law" of rectitude are really utilitarians in disguise because they are influenced to act by hope of reward or fear of punishment.[30]

Even a casual reading of Channing's works will reveal how closely his idea of the understanding—or reason, as he and the transcendentalists preferred to call it—parallels that of Price and of Thomas Reid, whose concept of the moral faculty is essentially the same as Price's.[31] Channing, as well as they, believed in a moral principle that was both intellectual and active, one that not only perceived the rightness of actions but also impelled the will to do that which was seen as right.[32]

Another key idea of Price and Reid to which Channing assented was the educability of the moral sense. Price believed, "There is no point of *moral* as well as *intellectual* improvement, beyond which we may not go by industry, attention, a due cultivation of our minds, and the help of proper advantages and opportunities."[33] Reid declared that the moral faculty was innate only "in germ" and therefore needed education and training in society to perfect it. Sentiments very much like these, and expressed in similar language, occupy a prominent place in most of Channing's utterances, public and private. Late in his career, an argument with Theodore Parker reveals that Channing stood fast although Parker, with the characteristic emphasis of the transcendentalists, questioned him about the infallibility of conscience and ridiculed his statement that conscience "must be educated, like the understanding."[34]

Just as Hutcheson revealed to Channing the infinite possibilities in man and Price confirmed for him God's end in creation as "the happiness of the virtuous and worthy,"[35] so in the Richmond period following Harvard, Adam Ferguson revealed to him that regeneration was a gradual and a social process. Following Montesquieu, Ferguson, in his *Essay on the History of Civil Society* (1767), argued that whatever progress man made must be achieved by his own exertions as a social being. "It should seem, therefore, to be the happiness of man," according to Ferguson, "to make his social dispositions the ruling spring of his occupations; to state himself as a member of a community, for whose general good his heart may glow with an ardent zeal, to the suppression of those personal cares which were the foundations of painful anxieties, fear, jealousy, and envy."[36]

By the time Channing returned to Newport after his Richmond sojourn, he was, as has been shown, convinced that virtue meant acting according to one's sense of duty. He had experienced the change of heart that is usually associated with religious conversion, and his new faith required more than secular morality to feed on.[37] At this crucial point in his spiritual development, one further influence was added to those already mentioned: his reacquaintance with Samuel Hopkins, now nearly eighty years old but still very bright and still very much the leader of the school of theological thought he had erected upon Edwards' New Light doctrines.

Channing described their relationship some years after the older man's death: "I was attached to Dr. Hopkins chiefly by his theory of disinterestedness. I had studied with great delight during my college life the philosophy of Hutcheson, and the Stoical morality, and these had prepared me for the Noble, self-sacrificing doctrines of Dr. Hopkins. . . . The idea of entire self-surrender to the general good was the strongest in his mind."[38] Though Channing could not accept Hopkins' "appalling theology," he conceded that it was founded on a basis of generosity: "True virtue, as he taught, was an entire surrender of personal interest to the benevolent purposes of God. . . . He called us to seek our own happiness as well as that of others, in a spirit of impartial benevolence; to do good to ourselves, not from self-preference, not from the impulse of personal desires, but in obedience to that sublime law, which requires us to promote the welfare of each and all within our influence."[39]

Channing also defended Hopkins' use of reason to support beliefs like predestination, which ran contrary to Channing's own. And in the same spirit, he commended Hopkins for important modifications of Calvinist teachings: "The doctrine that we are liable to punishment for the sin of our first parent, he wholly rejected; and not satisfied with denying the imputation of Adam's guilt to his posterity, he subverted what the old theology had set forth as the only foundation of divine acceptance, namely the imputation of Christ's righteousness or merits to the believer. The doctrine that Christ died for the elect only, found no mercy at his hands. He taught that Christ suffered equally for all mankind."[40]

Hopkins in turn became interested in the religious progress of Channing, but his death six months after the latter's ordination prevented his living to see what kind of minister Channing would make. Perhaps it was just as well. Although there was much in Channing's early religious thinking that resembled Hopkins' on the surface, the differences were even more significant. For while Hopkins and Channing, following the lead of the English rationalists and the Scotch moderates, dropped the idea of a sovereign Deity whose will required explicit obedience in favor of a benevolent Being who acted in accordance with an intelligible "nature of things," Hopkins looked back instead of to the future. His trust in divine benevolence was still insufficient to overcome his belief that human nature, being sinful and worthy of damnation, would bring men to eternal punishment. As a young minister Channing's evident piety and reliance upon the advice of his Grandfather Ellery, known Hopkinsian, may have led observers to conclude that he was a follower of New Light Calvinism; but the context of his preaching is certain to show that, except for the rational features of Hopkins' adaptation of Edwardean doctrine, Channing found the humanitarianism of Hutcheson and the Scotch ethical writers in general more to his liking because they drew no line between regenerate and unregenerate in their blueprint for future happiness and perfection.[41]

After the period of private study in Newport, Channing was able to complete his divinity studies at Harvard. Once more, David Tappan was his counselor and guide in theology, although the degree to which he influenced Channing can not be measured. It is sufficient to note, however, that Channing's recommendations at a later date for a course of study for divinity students reflect a continuing interest in Hutcheson, Ferguson, and Price.[42] At the time of his preparation for ordination and when Harvard was still a few years away from becoming Unitarian, Channing was well grounded in the Scottish philosophy that at the end of the decade would become practically official in both the College and the new Divinity School.[43]

In summary, the ideas that he had borrowed and made his own were very similar to the major conclusions of Thomas Reid, which also loom large in the thought of the other common-sense philosophers. Philosophy, for Reid, depends on scientific observation; and the primary object of it is self-consciousness and not the behavior of other men. The observation of self-consciousness, in turn, reveals principles that lie in the very constitution of the mind and that are not the product of experience since they are both prior to and independent of it. This self-consciousness also reveals that only intelligent agents can be efficient causes; matter can not be a cause but only a means in the hands of a real cause. Finally, the first principles of morals are not deduced from anything else because they are self-evident intuitions.[44]

Brief though it is, this outline is still sufficient to show why Channing found the Scottish philosophy so suitable to his needs and those of the age. For during his lifetime and for some time afterwards, the dualistic system of the Moderates provided exactly what Unitarian theology needed to meet the challenge of orthodox Calvinism and to grow and prosper. By the same token, the Calvinists, who were influenced by the same school to much the same degree as Channing was, lost the essence of the unique message they claimed for their brand of Christianity in an effort to temporize with the demands of the new age. Piety simply found less and less breathing room in an age in which Channing's humanitarianism began to assume ever-increasing stature. Although it must be granted that Channing's optimistic reorientation neglected some of the significant insights into human nature of Calvin— whose view of fallen man was, in some respects, much like that of the classic tragedians—still it is also true that it led to the evolutionary idealism of the social gospel and religious feeling with which his name and the half-century during which he worked are so closely associated.

Channing could attack both materialism and idealism as well as the pantheism to which emphasis on either could lead because of the clear-cut distinction between subject and object in the Scottish school. In *The Perfect Life*, he says, "From the very dawn of philosophy there have been schools which have held that the material universe has no existence but in the mind that thinks it. I am far from assenting to these speculations. . . . I do not say that the world exists in our thoughts *only*. But I do say that it derives its most interesting properties from the mind which contemplates it."[45] In his *Treatise on Man*, on the other hand, he refers to those views according to which "matter which seems to be the only reality vanishes, and nothing is left us in the outward world but the infinitely diversified agency of the creator. Matter and God become one, and Spirit which seems to many a shadow is the only existence distinct from the Divinity." But, he concludes, "I attach no importance to speculations of this character."[46]

If Channing tended to vacillate between dualism and idealism as far as matter and mind were concerned, he never hesitated to stand firmly on the dualism of the Creator and His creation. The Deity he preached remained transcendent from first to last; and His existence was revealed by reason and the Scriptures attested by Christian miracle.[47] Dualism also made it possible for him to invoke the genius of Bacon and Newton in riddling the mysteries of the material universe and at the same time affirm the identification of the human and Divine mind.[48] The universe was still God-centered, but for Channing the distance between man and the Throne was reduced to the point where it could be almost measured by self-consciousness. Almost but not quite: God was still transcendent, not immanent.

III *Rational Christianity*

Although the idea of man's worth and dignity as an individual capable of moral perfection is central to Channing's thought, his respect for human reason runs it a close second.

In reason, he says, lies man's true greatness, and the development of his intellect becomes his first duty, "for it is through soundness and honesty of intellect that he is to learn all other duties."[49]

Channing defines reason as "the highest faculty or energy of the mind." It has two principal functions: first, to grasp universal truths like causality, infinity, principles of right and wrong and then apply them to particular cases; and, second, to reduce these various thoughts to unity or consistency. "Its end and delight is harmony. . . . It corresponds to the unity of God and the universe, and seeks to make the soul the image and mirror of this sublime unity."[50] This view of the creative intellect is remarkably like that of Richard Price, for both agreed about the power of the mind to produce new ideas. And in large measure this creativity results from the intimate connection of the human and the Divine Mind, the former deriving from the latter and possessing "the power of approaching its original more and more through eternity." Separated from God, human reason would lose this capacity. "God delights to communicate himself; and therefore his greatness, far from inspiring contempt for human reason, gives it a sacredness, and opens before it the most elevating hopes. The error of men is, not that they exaggerate, but that they do not know or respect, the worth and dignity of their rational nature."[51]

And this error, declared Channing, is responsible for the fact that some religious beliefs show disdain for human reason. He was thinking of Calvinism, both in the form given it by Edwards and by his disciple, Samuel Hopkins. In a letter to Eloise Payne, a young friend of his Newport days, Channing described Calvinism's chilling and repressive aspects and then concluded: "On susceptible minds the influence of this system is always to be dreaded. If it be fully believed, I think there is ground for a despondence bordering on insanity."[52]

For Channing, as for Locke, whose *Reasonableness of Christianity* exercised an influence over Channing's earliest thoughts,[53] religion required reason's sanction. As he stated in his famous Baltimore sermon, "If religion be the shipwreck of understanding, we cannot keep too far from it."[54] At another time, he stated just as emphatically, "Christianity is a rational religion. Were it not so, I should be ashamed to profess it." And again, "I glory in Christianity because it enlarges, invigorates, exalts my rational nature. If I could not be a Christian without ceasing to be rational, I should not hesitate as to my choice."[55]

From the emphasis in this last statement, it would not be difficult to conclude—as did many of his contemporaries—that Channing was more rationalist than Christian. Some of his opponents were so aroused by his Baltimore sermon and the New York one in 1826 that they went to the extreme of labeling him a Deist. But before such an unwarranted conclusion is drawn, the relationship between reason and revelation in his thinking must be carefully studied.

There is no doubt that Channing believed reason was competent to deal with the question of revelation. "I am surer," he states, "that my rational nature is from God than that any book is an expression of his will. This light in my own breast is his primary revelation, and all subsequent ones must accord with it, and are, in fact, intended to blend with and brighten it."[56] Until proved, he continues, any "professed revelation from God" should be referred to the tests of reason. And among these, "none are more important than that moral law which belongs to the very essence and is the deepest conviction of the rational nature. Revelation, then, rests on reason, and in opposing it would act for its own destruction."[57]

Because of his rational nature Channing soon concluded that certain doctrines professed by his orthodox colleagues in the ministry could not possibly be part of God's revelation. He would not accept the Calvinist argument that a sovereign Being demanded acceptance of beliefs like total depravity, predestination, and the Trinity even though human intellect could not comprehend them. Such an argument, he declared, sets God against Himself—or against Reason, His image reflected in man.

Upon this premise, he induced Noah Worcester to become editor of *The Christian Disciple* in 1813. In his letter of invitation he told Worcester that, as far as the principles of Calvinism were concerned, "we are opposed to them, without censuring those who embrace those sentiments. We are opposed to that system particularly, inasmuch as it prostrates the independence of the mind, [and] teaches men that they are naturally incapable of discerning religious truth. . . ."[58] As it turned out, sweet reasonableness could not by itself turn away the wrath of orthodoxy, and Channing became embroiled in controversy, distasteful in itself because it smacked of sectarianism but especially displeasing to him because of his natural inclination to rely on free inquiry and avoid open conflict with its undertones of intolerance.

In his initial skirmish with orthodox spokesmen who tried to identify him and his associates with the materialistic and necessitarian beliefs of English Unitarians, Channing firmly disavowed these sentiments from which, he could truthfully say, the liberals would shrink "with as much aversion as from some of the gloomy doctrines of Calvin."[59] On the subject of the Trinity, he was no less firm in opposing the Calvinists on the grounds that their doctrine was both unscriptural and contrary to human reason. Although he tried to minimize as merely verbal his differences with the orthodox on this score, Channing certainly knew that he was striking at the very soul of the orthodox system. For Calvinism with its strain of Augustinian piety had reaped rich emotional harvests from its cosmic drama of magnificence highlighted by the Fall, the damnation of mankind, ransom by the Son of God, and a new birth; and Channing's refusal to recognize the role of Father, Son, and Holy Spirit in this drama could not be allowed to stand unquestioned.

By one of those ironies that so often illumines human experience, Channing might very easily have succumbed to the lure of Calvinism had it not been for the very doctrine upon which it placed so much reliance. Early in his ministerial career, depression induced by ill health tempted him to accept Calvinism but, in his own words, "the doctrine of the Trinity held me back."[60] There is no doubt, therefore, that his objections to the Trinity were fundamental, and it is not difficult to discover why he should have felt as he did.

For Channing it was clearly impossible to think of God the Father or of Christ as being other than a person, an ultimate entity incapable of either composition or division. By dividing God into three persons, the Trinitarian disrupted the unipersonality which Channing considered essential and made a mystery or unintelligible riddle out of the nature of both God and His Son.[61] In his denial of the Trinitarian belief, Channing joined reason and emotion because his premise that man can love only a being whom he can understand undergirded his conclusion that the unintelligible God of the Calvinist was unlovable. The Calvinist had to bear, therefore, the onus of subverting man's efforts to identify with the Divine Mind and to attain the moral perfection which is the chief glory of that Mind.[62]

At Baltimore, in the sermon on "Unitarian Christianity" that established the Unitarians as a distinct body within Congregationalism, Channing elaborated the basic principles over which the liberals and orthodox were to contend throughout the next two decades. To anyone familiar with what has already been delineated concerning his mental and moral development, those principles will sound familiar. Once again they included, on the positive side, the use of reason to test the Scriptures, belief in the unity of God and of Christ, and finally faith in the conscience of man and the moral perfection of God. "We consider no part of theology so important," said Channing, "as that which treats of God's moral character. . . . We believe that his almighty power is entirely submitted to his perceptions of rectitude; and this is the ground of our piety. . . ."[63] On the negative side is a denial of depravity, election, and the Anselmic doctrine of man's infinite guilt.

Only a year later he pressed home the same charges against the orthodox beliefs by asking, "How is it possible that men can hold these doctrines and yet maintain God's goodness and equity?" To the rejoinder that the ways of God are mysterious and above reason, he replied unequivocally, ". . . we maintain that God's attributes are intelligible, and that we can conceive as truly of his goodness and justice, as of these qualities in men. In fact, these qualities are essentially the same in God and man, though differing in degree, in purity, and in extent of operation."[64]

"Essentially the same"—this phrase contains the basis of every word and action of Channing's later life. Because he believed in man's essential godliness, he was also confident of man's potential goodness. There could no longer be any question of his split with the Calvinists when he held such divergent views of mankind. He was still most acceptable, however, to a young man like Emerson, who heard his defense of supernatural religion at Harvard and later wrote in his journal: "the highest species of reasoning upon divine subjects is rather the fruit of a sort of moral imagination, than of the 'Reasoning Machines,' such as Locke and Clarke and David Hume. Dr. Channing's Dudleian Lecture is the model of what I mean, and the faculty which produced this is akin to the higher flights of the fancy."[65]

Controversy naturally ensued from Channing's outspoken defense of the liberals' position, but he took little part in it. After his return from abroad in 1823, he began to reflect the influence of his *Wanderjahr* in Europe and of his visits with the English romantics. As he told his Federal Street congregation, ". . . my chief work in life is to act upon other minds, and to act through sympathy as well as instruction. . . ."[66] He was convinced now that "Men want and demand a more thrilling note, a poetry which pierces beneath the exterior of life to the depths of the soul. . . ."[67]

Perhaps this conviction motivated his address at the dedication of the Second Congregational Church in New York the following year. Although the title seems harmless and although he was reiterating for the most part what he had stated so effectively in Baltimore seven years before, his "Unitarian Christianity Most Favorable to Piety" aroused a storm of protest. The specific cause of orthodox ire was not Channing's testimony that Unitarianism works because it is true to man and God but rather his graphic image of a central gallows in the universe upon which Christ is hanged by his Father in order to atone for the sins of an audience whose members are compelled to watch the sacrificial victim die.[68] As Channing wrote to Lucy Aikin, "that production has drawn upon me more angry criticism than anything I have published."[69] Certainly, he had not intended to wound; but he had undeniably spoken in a way that "pierces to the depths of the soul" and lays open hidden sources of emotion that reasoned discourse is often powerless to touch.

But in "The Great Purpose of Christianity," an address

delivered at the installation of the Reverend M. I. Motte in 1828, Channing returned to his most characteristic theme. "The glory of Christianity," he exclaimed, "is, the pure and lofty action which it communicates to the human mind. . . . The highest existence in the universe is Mind; for God is mind; and the development of that principle which assimilates us to God, must be our supreme good."[70] In language reminiscent of the spirit breathed into Emerson's Divinity School Address, Channing then urged his listeners to cultivate a true freedom of mind. As he described his own philosophy of man thinking, he said, "I desire to escape the narrow walk of a particular church, and to live under the open sky, in the broad light, looking far and wide, seeing with my own eyes, hearing with my own ears, and following truth meekly but resolutely, however arduous or solitary be the path in which she leads."[71] He had many other things to say about man and his role in the universe, but they could all be summed up in his doctrine of self-reliance. The kingdom of Christ, he said, was in the human soul; and man must look for his blessings within himself and not from abroad.

His emphasis on human agency was bound to bring disapproval, but the response to the Motte Sermon was a whisper compared to the strident chorus that greeted his "Likeness to God" sermon at the ordination of Frederick Farley in the fall. "The idea of God, sublime and awful as it is," he declared, "is the idea of our own spiritual nature, purified and enlarged to infinity. . . . God is another name for human intelligence raised above all error and imperfection, and extended to all possible truth. . . . We see God around us, because he dwells within us."[72]

Although these were exalted views of humanity, they sounded like blasphemy to some of Channing's critics. One reviewer for the *Spirit of the Pilgrims* did not call Channing an out-and-out pantheist; but he did declare that his language, if it were not poetry, was close to that of pantheism and to universalism, too, for that matter.[73] On the surface, Channing's references to God in His creation do sound much like the later commonplaces of the transcendentalists; but his underlying beliefs are quite different. Like Emerson, Channing believed spirit was superior to matter and mind to body;

but he never regarded man as simply an emanation from the Godhead, as Emerson was to declare in *Nature,* nor did he consider nature simply a sign of spirit.[74] The personalism of his whole manner of thinking forbade submerging human identity in an over-soul; and the dualism of his common-sense mentors, Price and Reid, still carried greater weight than Berkeley's idealism although Channing conceded the latter's system might contain "some great latent truth, of which the European and Hindu intellect so generally at variance, have caught a glimpse."[75]

What really stood out in the Farley Sermon was not so much a preview of transcendental "infidelity" as a summary statement of Channing's concept of essential sameness. "God does not sustain a figurative resemblance to man," he declared. "It is the resemblance of a parent to a child, the likeness of a kindred nature."[76] Gone completely from his theology was the idea of God's sovereignty; the fatherhood of God and the sonship of man now constituted for him a divine relationship. Man was still a creature, and he would forever remain one; but Channing considered him capable of a spiritual progress to which there were no limits except those that he himself imposed.

Since progress of any kind depends upon freedom, it is not surprising that Channing chose to discuss "Spiritual Freedom" in his 1830 Election Sermon. Again, in anticipation of Emerson's "things are in the saddle and ride mankind" (Emerson was listening and could easily have found his inspiration here), Channing developed a magnificent list of mental freedoms and then warned his listeners that in a civilization growing increasingly materialistic, with pressure building up to consume human energies in petty mechanical operations, there was serious danger of "improved fabrics, but deteriorated men."[77]

As he read about the revolutions in Europe, he became convinced that "the mind is awakening to a consciousness of what it is, and of what it is made for."[78] His optimism permeated the discourse that he delivered in the summer of 1836 in his native Newport. The discourse on "Christian Worship" recalls the scenes of youth and early religious influences, but Channing did not allow nostalgia to keep him

from expanding upon the possibility of man's spiritual rise
to union with God. Two years later in the address on "Self-
Culture," he defined the religious principle in man as that
"power, which cannot stop at what we see and handle, at
what exists within the bounds of space and time, which seeks
for the Infinite, Uncreated Cause, which cannot rest till
it ascend to the Eternal, All-comprehending Mind."[79] On
both these occasions, Channing displays his characteristic
reverence for human reason, but there is also present an
emphasis that reminds one of the surge of the mystic toward
communion with God. The rationalism of Locke and the early
Arminian apologists of reason had now been translated into
a new idiom of faith and hope for an age of seemingly unlimited opportunities.

In his charge at the ordination of John Dwight in Northampton—the scene of Edwards' struggle to restrain the tide
flowing against Calvinism—Channing adjured the young
minister to remember that "something more than the action
of intellect is needed to secure to you a living knowledge of
Christian truth."[80] That something more was "a divine principle" within himself that could be unfolded if he would but
realize the potential of his likeness to God.

Standing at a point in his career when he knew that others
must carry on the main burden of work for the future, Channing prepared a 'Discourse on the Church," in which he
attempted to summarize his views of institutional religion.
From the very beginning of his career, he had demonstrated
his unwillingness to have anything to do with sectarianism
of any kind. Even when his own group had determined to
establish an American Unitarian Association, he had serious
reservations because of its possible effect in narrowing religious sentiment and excluding those who held honest difference of opinion. At various times he had explored the
possibilities of having laymen assume the duties of preaching
God's word because he did not want to close any avenue that
might serve both God and man more effectively. He had
encouraged all who believed that "God is, not was," and he
had constantly sought to breathe new life into his own
Church. Now he sought to describe a Church Universal that
would embrace "all sincere partakers of Christian virtue." No

institutional bonds would hold such a congregation together, he said, but their love to God and one another could do so. "Do not tell me," he exclaimed, "that I surrender myself to a fiction of imagination, when I say, that . . . all Christians and myself, form one body, one church, just as far as a common love and piety possess our hearts. . . . There *is* one grand, all-comprehending church; and if I am a Christian, I belong to it and no man can shut me out of it."[81] His ecumenical institution was the logical outcome of forty years of faithful service to the principles for which he had always stood: love of God, faith in man, and self-reliance.

CHAPTER 3

Social and Political Views

"THOUGH BORN in a revolution, I am anything but a revolutionist. My hope is in the regeneration of the world by the peaceful influence of Christianity and increased knowledge."[1] In these statements addressed to his long-time confidante, Lucy Aikin, Channing reveals both his propensity to avoid open conflict and his inheritance of general principles and rational Christianity from the Enlightenment. And yet when these words are put into the larger context of his career as one of the energizing spirits of the cultural life of the new nation that emerged after the American Revolution, they do not begin to tell the true story of William Ellery Channing's evolution as a social and political thinker. For certainly, his thought is not all of a piece from his college years at Harvard to his increasingly involved position in the reform movements of the late 1830's and early 1840's. Like his younger contemporary William Cullen Bryant, he had to emancipate himself from an early conservative Calvinistic and federalistic environment; like Bryant, too, he became in his later years an exponent of broad reform programs, involving world peace, emancipation from slavery, free trade, liberal education, and democratic practices in government. The passage of years marked his emergence as the leader of the opponents of religious orthodoxy.

As we have already seen, his boyhood in Newport and the years at Harvard show that Channing was keenly interested in politics and devoted to the principles of the Federalist party of which his father and grandfather were members.[2] Though his blood boiled, as an undergraduate, at the thought of French nationalism and although his heart was with John

Adams and the wearers of the black cockade, he did not, however, do any really serious thinking about politics until he was living in Richmond among people who held very different opinions about Adams, Jefferson, and the French. Then he wrote to a college chum: "I find this advantage from being in Virginia, that I must adopt no opinions on the measures of government without having grounds for it."[3]

Although he outlined in his letters back home a grandiose scheme for a socialistic paradise with communal property, Channing's position was fundamentally unchanged when he returned to Newport in 1800 to study for the ministry. As a matter of fact, he decided to forego profane studies so that he could concentrate on scriptural texts. He wrote in his journal: "Abstruse speculation on useless subjects will but waste my time. As I find myself full of prejudices on the subject of government and politics, I will lay them aside for a year. . . . History I will lay aside for the same time. Let me learn to be silent on subjects where I am ignorant."[4]

But after his ordination and during his early ministry when preoccupied with his pastoral duties and in conflict over the thought of his unworthiness to do God's work, he nevertheless found time for political theorizing. Since by now he was intrenched in his rationalistic bias toward broad general principles, he began to reexamine ideas previously left unquestioned in order to build a "science" of government.

I *Purpose of Government*

The purpose of political institutions, he had written from Richmond to his friend William Shaw, is to "improve and morally elevate human nature."[5] On this point he never wavered, although he would become less sanguine concerning the efficacy of government as experience revealed to him the shortcomings of political systems. But as a true son of the Enlightenment, the young minister found it eminently reasonable to think of political, social, and moral ideas as being interrelated and established on the same "natural" principles. Many years later, in a draft of his introduction to a projected work on "The Principles of Moral, Religious, and Political Science" (one of the many abortive attempts before, during, and after the Enlightenment to find "a science of human nature"[6]) he wrote: "All our inquiries in morals, religion, and politics must begin with human nature. . . . It is the want of a true science of our nature, that has vitiated all past systems of government, morals, and religion."[7]

Consequently, it was to be expected that a Channing still under the domination of Calvinism would support the Federalists' belief that men, because of their depravity, should be carefully controlled. "We carry our own shame on our foreheads," he wrote in 1804. "Most of our civil institutions grow out of our corruptions. We cannot live without mutual dependence, and yet we are forced to hedge each other round, to bind and shackle each other, institute inquiries. . . ."[8] But thirty years later, although positively convinced by this time of the human potential for perfectibility, Channing could still declare that "society has instituted government, erected the tribunal of justice . . . put the sword into the hand of the magistrate, and pledged its whole force to his support" in order "to guard reputation, property, and life."[9] In this statement he still recognizes the necessity of the coercive power of government, but the admission now is a measure of the distance between his ideal and the actual state of mankind.

Federalist though he undoubtedly was for a time, Channing never shared the antidemocratic prejudice of Federalist leaders like Fisher Ames, who felt that Jefferson with his ideas of territorial expansion was rushing the States "like a comet into infinite space" or, worse still, making them too democratic for liberty to be preserved. Nor did Channing's views of human nature ever reach the depths of agreeing with Hamilton's view—"Your people, sir, is a great beast!" But he was very much the Federalist in his youthful hatred of the French Revolution and of everything it produced. A more mature judgment of the French nation and of the causes of its Revolution would have to await greater knowledge of European history and a change in political theory. He finally broke with the Federalist viewpoint in 1829 because he found a lack of faith in human nature manifested by the leaders of the party. As he put it, "the Federalists as a body wanted a just confidence in our national institutions."[10]

From the beginning of his public career, then, Channing believed in considering man's moral development when trying to assign the proper functions to society and government. As long as he accepted the tenets of Calvinism, he found it logical to support the coercive aspects of government. But when he began to admit the possibility of human improvement, he found it necessary to modify his theories.

After war had been declared on Great Britain in 1812, Channing addressed his congregation about the citizen's responsibility in times of trial or danger. Government, he told his people, is "the great security for social happiness." It is "a divine institution, essential to the improvement of our nature, the spring of industry and enterprise, the shield of property and life, the refuge of the weak and oppressed."[11] He makes mention not of the negative force of government, but of its positive aspects of promoting economic well-being on the one hand and of protecting human rights on the other. In 1820 he extended this proposition by declaring, "Man is the only glory of a country, and it is the advancement and unfolding of human nature which is the true interest of a state."[12] Coupled with this statement is the admonition that the state must not place any restraints on its citizens except those demanded by the public good. The shift in emphasis from the coercive to the benevolent aspects of government is noteworthy.

But of even greater significance is another aspect of this idea that occurs constantly in Channing's writings and public addresses after 1820. "We do not want government to confer on us positive blessings," he states, "but simply to secure to us the unobstructed exercise of our powers in working out blessings for ourselves."[13] Like Jefferson before him, he was underlining the need for social and political individualism; in his own right, he was asserting the harm that the concept of a welfare state could do to individual initiative. The greatest political blessing to any people, he emphasized, is liberty; for moral progress—and hence progress of any kind—can be accomplished only by free individuals. "Virtue, from its very nature, cannot be a product of what may be called the direct operation of government; that is, of legislation."[14]

By ruling out "the direct operation of government," Channing evidently believed he had answered Americans like Daniel Webster who felt that government should protect the interest of people with the largest economic stake in society. In 1822 he vigorously argued that "the poor, weak, helpless, suffering, are the first objects for the care of government. . . . The very protection of property may crush a large mass of the community, may give the rich a monopoly in land, may take from the poor all means of action."[15] If the wording of these remarks is somewhat unfortunate—leading to the impression that the State is a kind of welfare agency— their context makes it clear that Channing is against special privilege for any class. His regard for the underprivileged is solely for the protection of their rights as free citizens. Furthermore, unlike the Social Darwinists of a later era, Channing believed that the social classes owed much to one another: "The best condition of society is that in which all ranks, classes, orders, are intimately connected and associated. . . . All men cannot be equal in all respects; but the high should feel their elevation to be a motive and obligation to labor for inferiors."[16]

II *Moral Renovation*

By the end of Channing's second decade in the ministry, his hopes that government might live up to his ideal began to dim. Experience was simply against the realization of Jefferson's "blessings of liberty" for all; instead, examples were multiplying of the concentration of power among the wealthy and of a worsening of social conditions among those less favored. And so upon his return from Europe in 1823, he told his people: "I expect less and less from revolutions, political changes, violent struggles,—from public men on public measures,—in a word, from any outward modification of society." Henceforth his hope for world improvement would rest upon *moral renovation* because "corrupt institutions will be succeeded by others equally, if not more, corrupt, whilst the root or principle lives in the heart of individuals and nations."[17]

This program of "internal" reform which Channing followed

until his death has led at least one eminent modern historian to accuse him of "sabotaging the liberal impulses of his day."[18] But such an accusation is unwarranted because of its over-emphasis on Channing's unawareness of social change and its primary failure to recognize the limitations of purely "external" reform. But it is certainly true that as Channing began to concentrate more and more on what he called "moral power," his skepticism about external change increased; and this was especially noticeable about areas where government was intended to produce desirable social goals. Writing of prison reform, for example, he asks rhetorically: "Can legislation do much toward reforming men? Has not the power of government in this, as in everything, been overrated?"[19]

Furthermore, such questions demonstrate how prominently the subject of power figured in his thoughts at this time. In his second article on Napoleon, he defined three different kinds of power: inward, or power over oneself; power over outward *things*; and power over other men. The last kind he discussed at length since he was trying to explain the nature of Napoleon's rule over men and nations; but his remarks have even larger application, for they concern his attitude toward political matters in general.

Power over other men may be used for good or evil, he declares. When it is manifested in "the influence of a good and great mind over other minds," it becomes spiritualized and no other force can compare with it. But when it is used to further selfish ambition by reducing other men to "slave and machine," it works the greatest harm. In the past priest and ruler have been the chief abusers:

> The influence of almost every political and religious institution has been to make man abject in mind, fearful, servile, a mechanical repeater of opinions which he does not try, and a contributor of his toil, sweat, and blood, to governments which never dreamed of the general weal as their only legitimate end.[20]

By the time, then, of Andrew Jackson's election to the presidency, Channing had become disenchanted with the idea of governmental benevolence. The chief influence of government was negative; it was like a wall around the country—"a needful protection, but reaping no harvests, ripening no fruits." Time was "when sovereigns fixed prices and wages, regulated industry and expense," but, said Channing, "we have learned that men are their own best guardians, that property is safest under its owner's care, and that, generally speaking, even great enterprises can better be accomplished by the voluntary association of individuals than by the state."[21]

The following year his article "The Union," published just two months after Jackson had taken office, reiterated his belief that "the highest political good, liberty, is negative." Since liberty is the reason for laws being enacted, they "should be plain and few, intended to meet obvious wants" and "such as common minds may comprehend."[22] Here would seem to be an eighteenth-century man speaking. Actually Channing's emphasis on truths that carry their own self-evidence places him among the anti-Lockeans who had moved away from empiricism toward intuitional sources of truth.[23] If Channing spoke with almost sublime confidence of the ability of the individual to "achieve his happiness by his own unfettered powers," his trust was sanctioned by proof that he found within his own breast. And yet his thinking on social and political subjects still carried echoes of Adam Ferguson's *Essay on the History of Civil Society* which had been a favorite since Harvard days. For Ferguson had also believed that "the strength of a nation is derived from the character, not from the wealth, nor from the multitudes of its people";[24] and he had written that just as the public good was the goal of individuals so, too, "the happiness of individuals is the great end of civil society."[25]

In any case, Channing's public utterances during the early 1830's seldom grapple with the crises, major or minor, that make the Age of Jackson such a stirring period in American history. His correspondence to friends at home and abroad touches upon political personalities and party factions and alludes briefly to matters like the tariff and the National Bank, but none of these subjects is treated with the thoroughness he was accustomed to giving religious topics. He told Lucy Aikin, for example, that President Jackson was re-

sponsible for turning "our prosperity into commercial dis-
tress"[26] even though a short time before he had found it
necessary to write his friend Congressman Nathan Appleton
for some literature on the bank system because he did not
understand the problems involved. Somewhat earlier he had
asked Appleton to send him a copy of a speech of Senator
John Calhoun. "I seldom read debates," he wrote, "but the
constitutional questions discussed in these speeches are so
important, and some of them are attended with so much
difficulty that I am anxious to possess the best means of
forming a correct judgment."[27]

His intentions were good; but he had neither time nor
energy (he was constantly beset by ill health during these
years[28]); and—if the truth be told—he lacked the strong incentive necessary to become engrossed in the immediate social
problems of the national scene. He was, of course, desirous of
forming "broad, general principles" upon which to base his
preaching; but, like his disciple Emerson later on, he had
"quite other slaves to free . . . to wit, imprisoned spirits,
imprisoned thoughts." Thus he could not involve himself in
social and political problems like his friends George Bancroft,
Josiah Quincy, and Edward Everett, who were finding the
wine of politics a heady draught indeed.

Yet his interest in national and international affairs and
in the men who made the news did not wane. As he told
Miss Aikin, "The world is not, as yet, so rich in superior
minds that we can afford to part with one."[29] Consequently,
he wanted to be certain to give just due to "intellectual greatness and distinguished virtue." He even asked her help to
overcome his besetting fault of overlooking details and judging
too much by general principles.[30]

Perhaps this fault was largely responsible for an ambivalence
in his judgment of individual personalities. In general he
supported the Federalist and Whig leaders, yet he had reservations about their complete allegiance to liberal principles
and the welfare of the individual. Even Washington, whom
he described as "the most remarkable man of modern times,"
belonged to the party that "in some respects failed of its duty
to the cause of Union and of freedom."[31] Similarly, although
he granted that the Whigs included the best men, he warned

the new party in 1837 that it would fail unless it supported the laboring classes and avoided "partiality to the moneyed class."[32] Three years later he foresaw trouble because the Whigs controlled so much wealth; and, at the start of Tyler's administration, he referred to them as "blind conservatives."[33]

But the Democrats offered little hope either. Jefferson was "a man of genius" who possessed "the most generous theory of human rights," but "he stood alone." His successor, Andrew Jackson, had preserved peace by his "iron will and invincible firmness," but subservient followers had tempted him to "executive usurpation" and to buy favor with patronage.[34] Neither party promised much for future progress: the Whigs were "threatened with dissolution," and "Would the Democrats break up too," there might be a chance to start afresh.[35] Such was not Emerson's feeling because, although tending to look with the same jaundiced gaze upon the passing carnival, he nevertheless hoped that "this rank rabble party, Jacksonianism of the country . . . may root out the hollow dilettantism of our cultivation. . . ."[36] Channing could not agree. As a party the Democrats were no ·better than any other. "I am a thorough republican," he insisted;[37] but after thirty years of following the course of party politics, he had become convinced that party membership must lead to "party spirit, the worst enemy of free governments."[38]

Until men themselves improved in wisdom and virtue, Channing believed their political institutions would remain imperfect. This was a general judgment embracing all forms of government; but the fact that a popular government had its evils and that "a people, on the whole, are poor rulers" did not, for a moment, keep him from asserting that the people govern "far better than kings and aristocracies."[39] Believing that only democratic governments were founded "in natural right" (as did Jefferson and countless other optimists of the Enlightenment), Channing unequivocally opposed aristocracy because it was established on the false principle of hereditary rather than personal distinctions and because it tended inevitably to distort human worth. And since the direct result of hereditary rank was to make men worth very little, he could see no reason why aristocrats themselves

should not lead the effort to pull down aristocratic governments.[40]

To have confidence in this degree of human disinterestedness must have strained even Channing's sublime trust. But
more than most of his contemporaries, he welcomed the
"stern teacher, revolution" and judged its lessons worthwhile
in spite of the great price in human suffering paid for them.
The people would have to rise in spite of their leaders. Proof
of this fact came from Europe in 1830 when the revolutionary
spirit flamed in France, Belgium, and Poland. The success
of the July Revolution in Paris made him jubilant, but his
anxiety for the Poles found no relief. After their defeat by
Nicholas' imperial forces, he sent what money he could spare
and urged his friends abroad to awaken world opinion to the
evils of Czarist oppression.[41] At best these were inadequate
means to assuage the grief of patriots, but they would help
until time itself brought full remedy.

And freedom's hour was rapidly approaching. In feudal
times, Channing conceded, aristocrats had served a useful
function as leaders and protectors of their people. But as he
counseled Lucy Aikin, when she made even temperate de-
fenses of her English system, the present state of society
had changed so drastically that the aristocracy would have
to find either an "equivalent relation" to it or pass out of
existence.[42] He thought it was unlikely—despite Miss Aikin's
assurance that the barriers of old, blind custom were breaking
down in England—that the privileged classes could long
preserve themselves. "I believe," he wrote her with some
vehemence, "that the tendencies of aristocracy are hostile
to those of Christianity and civilization . . . and that it is out
of place and must be a perpetual spring of jealousy and
disunion in times like the present. . . ."[43]

On the other hand, Channing's abhorrence of monarchy
and aristocracy did not blind him to the weaknesses of democratic societies. "I wish the people to govern no farther
than they must," he said shortly before his death. "I honor
the passion for power and rule as little in the people as
in a king. It is a vicious principle, exist where it may . . . the
unfettered multitude is not dearer to me than the unfettered

king." In the same vein, he wrote Dr. Francis Wayland, president of Brown University: "The doctrine, that 'the majority ought to govern,' passes with the multitude as an intuition, and they have never thought how far it is to be modified in practice, and how far the application of it ought to be controlled by other principles."[44]

One of these principles was undoubtedly fitness to vote. For, despite his belief in a democratic suffrage, Channing was firmly convinced that no one should be given the elective franchise until he had been instructed in the principles of his government and in his duties as a citizen.[45] One of the major aims of the public schools, he declared, should be to teach citizenship; and the admission to voting privilege should be preceded by an examination of all candidates and celebrated as "the grand national festival."[46] Part of his concern was to prevent the rising tide of immigrants, who were totally ignorant of American institutions, from falling easy prey to power-hungry politicians;[47] but he was also striving to educate the public to accept higher standards for all classes of voters.

Public opinion, Channing knew, could exert even greater force than the power of aristocracy. Fully aware of the pressures to conform in a republic, he never ceased to deprecate what he called the people's "force as a mass." The great danger of the power of opinion, he declared in 1830 in his sermon on "Spiritual Freedom," is that it "grows into a despotism, which more than all things, represses original and free thought, subverts individuality of character, reduces the community to a spiritless monotony, and chills the love of perfection."[48]

"The idea of a national interest prevails in the minds of statesmen," he continued, "and to this it is thought that the individual may be sacrificed. But I would maintain, that the individual is not made for the state so much as the state for the individual."[49] The chief end of government, as he had stated ten years before, was to provide the proper sphere for man to realize his individuality; but in saying this, Channing did not mean to belittle service to the state. "There is a beautiful harmony between the good of the state and the moral freedom and dignity of the individual," he asserts.[50]

By carrying out the duties enjoined upon him by his God-given rights as an individual, the citizen develops his character and thereby fulfills the end for which the state is designed.

Channing believed that duties and rights stood together because he identified man's origin with his end. Man, he argued, was created with rights that had to be exercised if he were to become what God had destined him to be—a "Rational, Moral Immortal Being" with all his godlike faculties unfolded.[51] To the notion that society came into being as a result of social compact, Channing was strongly opposed. "Society is of earlier and higher origin. It is God's ordinance, and answers to what is most godlike in our nature."[52] Nor did he like the idea that in forming civil society, "the individual surrenders a part of his rights." It would be more correct, he claimed, to say that "he adopts new modes of securing them."[53] To obtain justice and protection of property, for example, man willingly submits to civil laws and taxation.

But what about the natural rights that figure so prominently in Channing's social and political thinking? The fullest exposition of them occurs in his article on "Slavery," where his defense of every man's right to his own person and of human dignity itself compelled him to organize his ideas on the subject more clearly and thoroughly than ever before. All human rights may, he declares, be comprised in one—"the right, which belongs to every rational being, to exercise his powers for the promotion of his own and others' Happiness and Virtue."[54] From this "great fundamental right of human nature," certain particulars may be derived; and among these Channing mentions specifically the right of every man

1. To exercise and invigorate his intellect.
2. To inquire into his duty, and to conform himself to what he learns of it.
3. To use the means, given by God and sanctioned by virtue, for bettering his condition.
4. To be respected according to his moral worth.
5. To be regarded as a member of the community to which he belongs, and to be protected by impartial laws.
6. To be exempted from coercion, stripes, and punishment, as long as he respects the rights of others.

7. To [receive] an equivalent for his labor.
8. To sustain domestic relations, to discharge their duties, and to enjoy the happiness which flows from fidelity to these and other domestic relations.[55]

Although this list was not intended to be complete and although Channing did not attempt to offer proof of his deductions, he did perform an important service by making explicit what had hitherto been simply assumed. Furthermore, he was establishing the rationale upon which his belief in democracy rested as well as an explanation of his distrust of "the unfettered multitude." For him democracy could never mean unbridled majority rule. Like most of the founding fathers, he believed in a people governing itself under a constitution that provided for keeping the popular will within bounds. As a man of truth and candor, he was compelled to say, however, that although "Democracy, considered in itself, is the noblest form of government, and the only one to satisfy a man who respects himself and his fellow-creatures . . . if its actual operation be regarded . . . it works very imperfectly."[56]

CHAPTER 4

Social Reformer

BOTH EARLY AND LATE, Channing looked from his corner upon America and the larger worlds of England and Europe and discovered how imperfect human society can be. In every instance, his response was to search for a solution; but he reversed the usual process by progressing from conservatism to liberalism as he looked for and found different answers.

As a youthful college graduate, enthusiasm tempted him to visionary schemes of reaching Utopia by the simple expedient of changing the external forms of society. As the young Federal Street minister, he thought more practically of a Christian social gospel that would meet the wants of the sick, the poor, and the uneducated.[1] As a European traveler returned home with renewed vision and hope, he sought a social revolution based on moral renovation. Finally as Dr. Channing, seasoned by debate and discussion of religious principles and tempered in the crucible of antislavery, he preached a doctrine of self-culture based on a sublime faith in man, "a wonderful being, endowed with incomprehensible grandeur, worthy of his own incessant vigilance and care, worthy to be visited with infinite love from heaven."[2]

I *The Goal of Perfection*

In the beginning of his ministry, Channing decided that the perfection of character should be his main goal. "We should preach," he said, "that we may make men perfect Christians; perfect, not according to the standard of the world, but according to the law of Christ; perfect in heart and in life, in solitude and in society, in the great and in the common concerns of life."[3] After nearly two decades of experience, he was only more convinced that "Society is the school in which the heart is trained for the Creator"; and his defense of the antislavery cause rested upon his belief that "The spiritual principle in man is what entitles him to our brotherly regard."[4] Nearing the end of his career, he could say with a sincerity born of his whole life's work, "I know but one elevation of a human being, and that is elevation of Soul. Without this, it matters nothing where a man stands or what he possesses; and with it he towers, he is one of God's nobility, no matter what place he holds in the social scale."[5]

Channing's lifelong devotion to moral worth as the starting point for social reform is a natural outgrowth of his principles as a rational Christian. Since religion meant character-building by the individual and since he was formed by society, Channing believed in actively promoting social reform. But he put his own peculiar stamp upon philanthropy. As George Bancroft described it, "*Moral Power* was to him the Egeria that dictated, the energy that accomplished reform."[6] For this very reason, some of his contemporaries (even some of his followers) and most modern critics have concluded that Channing was not interested in practical, material social measures. Such a conclusion is unwarranted because Channing agreed that the improvement of environment could be beneficial to man's spiritual development as well as detrimental. But he made it clear that material goods could never be anything but the means to, and therefore of only secondary importance in, human progress.[7] The solid theistic foundation of his particular brand of humanism is responsible for such an emphasis and accounts also for the rejection of his ideas by modern humanists, who praise him as a personality but turn away from his conclusions because their gods are not his God.

Since knowledge was indispensable to any kind of progress, Channing believed that moral growth depended upon a community's success in educating its citizenry. "There is no office higher than that of a teacher of youth," he wrote, "for there is nothing on earth so precious as the mind, soul, character of the child."[8] His interest in the work of teachers like

Eloise Payne, Elizabeth Peabody, Dorothea Dix, Bronson Alcott, and Horace Mann and his close ties with George Ticknor, Edward Everett, and George Bancroft reveal not only the usual role of counselor and moral supporter but also an active and original thinker. Long before modern theorists were to explore and test their "discoveries," he anticipated ability grouping, acceleration of gifted students, and the importance of linguistic studies.[9] He foresaw clearly the major role adult education would have to play in a democracy, and he made his own parish an arena of experiment for "conversation meetings."[10] No respecter of persons, he believed that education should be given to anyone who could benefit from it. "The strongest argument for education is found in the nobleness of the human faculties," he said, "and the poor bring with them into being the same faculties with the opulent. Nature knows none of our arbitrary distinctions."[11] Therefore he worked constantly for better education for indigent boys, for tradesmen and mechanics, and for those interested in business.

II *The Great Evils*

Underlying all this effort was Channing's hope that mass education might lead to a shortening of the drudgery most men endured to satisfy their "animal wants." He regarded intemperance as a great evil but recognized that its moral aspects were joined to the physical drives of men and women who looked to alcohol for relief from their brutalizing work or from the boredom of empty lives.[12] In his typical fashion, after considering how addicts might be acted upon both inwardly and outwardly to become temperate, he concluded that, while it was helpful to reduce the pressures that drive people to drink, it was more important to increase their powers of resistance by educating them to find release and expression in higher pleasures, such as music, drama, and literature.[13]

Although Channing found intemperance a great moral evil because it led to "the voluntary extinction of reason,"[14] he viewed war as incalculably worse because it "is the concentration of all human crimes."[15] Hating war with a passion, partly, one supposes, because its dark shadow filled his world from beginning to end, but primarily because it let loose unimaginable moral and physical devastation, he wrote sermons about it in 1812, 1814, 1816, in 1835, and again in 1838. His letters often allude to the subject, and even the "Introductory Remarks" to his *Works* contains a word of explanation for his preoccupation with such a distasteful subject.

From first to last, Channing's views of war are the same. "The field of battle," he exclaimed, "is a theatre, got up at immense cost, for the exhibition of crime on a grand scale."[16] No war of aggression can ever be justified, but there may be times when a defensive war becomes necessary to preserve the existence or freedom of a country after all other means have been exhausted.[17] But, he solemnly warns: "If any action on earth ought to be performed with trembling . . . it is a declaration of war."[18]

When Lucy Aikin received a copy of these remarks, she raised the obvious questions concerning the difficulty of drawing a line between "offence and defence" and pointed out that expediency and utility would operate to confuse the issue.[19] Though no record exists of Channing's reply, the critic is captious who concludes that he had not anticipated such difficulty. Nor does it make good sense to argue that Channing never faced up to the problem of war because he was not a pacifist or never found a solution to wars. The pacifist may satisfy his individual conscience, but he does not solve war. And who, it may be asked, *has found* a way to eliminate wars? Miss Aikin knew, despite her criticism, that Channing's sermon on war was one of his "best services to the interests of human nature," and she told him so.[20]

But preaching was not enough for Channing: he had to be active in social enterprises. Taking a cue from Noah Worcester, he invited to his parsonage a group interested in peace; and, through his urging and counsel, they formed the Peace Society of Massachusetts on December 28, 1815. It was the first society of its kind in America. Later, Channing helped to promote its cause by addressing to the Senate and House in Washington a memorial urging inquiry into methods whereby peace might be promoted at home and abroad.[21]

In addition to his work for peace, he investigated conditions in prisons and other public institutions and advocated reforms based on humanitarian principles. Through his work with various agencies in Boston, he became acquainted with John Cheverus, the Catholic Bishop of Boston who was desirous of alleviating misery and unhappiness wherever he could.[22] Bishop Cheverus was beloved by Protestants and Catholics alike, but he and Channing were especially drawn to each other by much the same views of philanthropy. They worked side by side until Cheverus was recalled to a bishopric in France.

In the mid-twenties, wealth, immigration, and growth were making significant changes in the Boston that Channing had known when he first arrived from Newport. Increasing industrialization and urbanization were complicating the old problems of pauperism and crime, and laboring people were just beginning to realize the effectiveness of organization in securing better working conditions.[23] Channing followed intently the efforts of state committees like the one on poor relief, which was headed by his good friend and parishioner, Josiah Quincy;[24] but he also looked for new and dramatic ways to bring about reform. Taking exception to the charge that "romantic expectations of great changes in society will do more harm than good," he insisted that the outstanding quality of human nature is its "susceptibleness of improvement."[25]

His conviction that moral reform depended upon a prior awakening of conscience and a quickening of religious inspiration now distinguished his hopes for society from his student dreams of a golden age of justice, equality, and fraternity to be achieved either by changing the world completely or by quitting it. When he became chairman of a committee to recommend ways to improve the youth of Boston, he found his answers naturally in a program of increased educational opportunities. His committee gave preference to moral and religious instruction, as might be expected; but it did not overlook practical suggestions. Out of its report came an investigation of the mechanics' institutes in Britain and Scotland in order to discover better ways to instruct Boston apprentices in the scientific principles of their trades.[26]

The older he grew, the more Channing looked to the less

privileged members of society—the poor and the working classes—to bring about needed social improvements. Unlike his fellow countryman, James Fenimore Cooper, who believed that the welfare of society depended upon a class of gentlemen, Channing put his trust in the individuality of the common man. "That the Many are not to be called to think, study, improve their minds, because a privileged few are intended by God to do their thinking for them" appeared to him the worst of prejudices.[27] The most important part of any society, he told Lucy Aikin, is the people, simply because there are so many of them. An obvious truth, but few believed it, or even understood it—the people themselves least of all. Viewing himself as "a leveller," he wrote Joanna Baillie that he would redress the imbalance of social classes "by elevating the low, by raising from a degrading indigence and brutal ignorance the laboring multitude."[29]

The passion for wealth and the worship of property seemed to Channing to be twin evils strangling the best impulses among all classes of society. In the competition for success, he saw that many were necessarily psychologically maimed: "Just as far as wealth is the object of worship, the measure of men's importance, the badge of distinction, so far there will be a tendency to self-contempt and self-abandonment among those whose lot gives them no chance of its acquisition."[30] But the poor were not the only victims. The so-called highest classes were so blinded by "the idolatry of wealth" that they lacked a perception of spiritual excellence as well as "the consciousness of their solemn obligations to the less favored classes of society."[31]

Since there was little hope that people in high places would take the initiative to right social wrongs, Channing concentrated throughout the twenties and early thirties on educating the poor and working classes to help themselves. With Joseph Tuckerman as his lieutenant, he established the Ministry at Large in 1826 and watched its progress carefully as Tuckerman carried on the work among Boston's poorest citizens.[32] Though the effort to bring religion into the homes of those who did not belong to any church body was well intentioned, Channing had to admit that it bore little fruit.[33] Orestes Brownson's work with laboring groups was no more successful, although Channing attributed the failures to Brownson's adoption of "a philosophical style not suited to them."[34]

Despite these signs that moral progress would be slow and difficult, Channing remained convinced throughout the 1830's that the proper course was to upgrade the working class; but he never extended the false hope that the working man would ever be relieved of the necessity of manual labor, an incentive to which less scrupulous enthusiasts sometimes resorted in order to get support.[35] Perhaps he was naïve in thinking that the rich would be willing to support educational plans without taxation; still he believed "if . . . the enlightened among the laboring classes and their enlightened friends will set in motion a system of improvement which promises good and great results, the rich will not be found wanting."[36]

Some modern sociological critics take strongest issue with reformers like Channing at this very point. Accustomed as many of them are to conceive of social justice in terms of the removal of physical impediments to pleasure and happiness, they find Channing's rejection of materialistic explanations of what is wrong with society hard to accept. To them, the following statement proves positively that Channing was blind both to the realities of poverty and to the privileges of his own class:

> That some of the indigent among us die of scanty food, is undoubtedly true; but vastly more in this community die from eating too much, than from eating too little . . . many shiver from want of defences against the cold; but there is vastly more suffering among the rich from absurd and criminal modes of dress . . . than among the poor from the deficiency of raiment . . . the poor are often over-worked, but they suffer less than many among the rich who have no work to do, no interesting object to fill up life, to satisfy the cravings of man for action.[37]

To conclude from such a passage that he must have been insensitive to the problems of others is reasonable only if one overlooks Channing's unceasing efforts to relieve wretchedness, or if one rejects the Christian principle that salvation may come easier to the weary and heavy-laden than to those who are blessed with worldly possessions. Channing no longer harbored the Enlightenment dream of bringing heaven to earth when he wrote these remarks; his purpose was rather to prepare men to leave earth for heaven. Those who charge him with blindness or worse may have faulty vision themselves; or perhaps by limiting their seeing to earthly objects, they lose sight of the vision of Channing's *Ultima Thule*.

III   *Abolition*

Although he did not lose track of the various reform activities in which he had formerly engaged, Channing devoted his major energies during the last ten years of his life to the subject of slavery. Denounced by his own parishioners as an Abolitionist but regarded at times by the Abolitionists themselves as an open enemy, Channing proved his moral and physical courage time and again by following the path of conscience into unpopular causes. His correspondence during these late years shows how wholeheartedly he involved himself in the antislavery cause once he had decided where his duty lay.[38] Always zealous to have his views supported by evidence, though he sometimes was less thorough than he might have wished to be, Channing surpassed himself in acquiring authoritative information about slavery from such worthies as Justice Joseph Story, Henry Clay, Daniel Webster, and John Quincy Adams. Because of this careful research, his several writings about this subject carry a cogency and purposefulness sometimes lacking in his other writing.

Although Channing discussed slavery as early as 1826[39] and sufficiently often and frankly in the early 1830's to cause some coolness to develop toward him among his wealth parishioners, who disliked hearing him link wealth with slavery, it was not until 1835 that he went publicly on record with his pamphlet "Slavery." From then on, he lent all the force of his considerable reputation to the antislavery movement; but he never became an Abolitionist, principally because he objected to the extreme measures Abolitionists sometimes advocated.[40] Some grew impatient with him because they failed to understand that his love of reform was always balanced by his love of order, but they—Lydia Maria Child was one of them —learned through better acquaintance, as did she, "that it was justice to *all*, not popularity for himself, which made him so cautious."[41]

As his friend George Bancroft realized, Channing's doctrine about slavery "lay at the very heart and core of his whole system of theology."[42] His belief in the importance of every human being coupled with his doctrine of natural rights and his hatred of the abuse of power led him to view slavery, even in the abstract, as a great moral evil; but his experiences with it in Richmond and St. Croix proved that, in its most humane guise, it was still an odious crime against humanity. However, true to the last to his faith that men are not naturally evil, he continued to distinguish between the slaveholder's crime and his character because he did not believe that men could always "be interpreted by their acts or institutions."[43]

In his "Slavery," Channing attempted first to show that man cannot be justly held or used as property. "He cannot be property in the sight of God and justice, because he is a Rational, Moral, Immortal Being; because created to unfold godlike faculties, and to govern himself by a Divine Law written on his heart, and republished in God's word. . . . Such a being was plainly made for an End in Himself. He is a person, not a Thing. He is an End, not a mere Instrument or Means."[44] Next, he argued that man's rights cannot be abrogated by man-made law because they derive from God rather than from society. The rights which are sacred above all others are those which enable a man to unfold his moral and intellectual nature. Slaves are given no such opportunity.

Finding slavery evil "from its own nature," Channing listed a formidable number of examples of its violation of human rights. He charted its ruinous effects on both slave and master and concluded that "an institution so founded in wrong, so imbued with injustice, cannot be made a good."[45] When he came to the means of removing slavery, he emphasized that moral principle must guide any course of action; but he opposed colonization because it would "perpetuate the evil without end."[46] He preferred a system of graduation to immediate emancipation, but he rejected the argument that intermarriage would result from emancipation. "Can this objection be urged in good faith?" he asked. "Can this mixture go on faster or more criminally than at the present moment? Can the slaveholder use the word 'amalgamation' without a blush?"[47]

The appearance of Channing's pamphlet excited various kinds of censure and blame. Garrison denounced it as "utterly destitute of any redeeming, reforming" power, and Sarah Grimké wrote a bill of particulars disagreeing heartily with Channing's subtle distinction between wrongdoing and the wrongdoer.[48] The most virulent attack came from James T. Austin, attorney general of Massachusetts and a distinguished member of Channing's own congregation, who charged him with "*the doctrine of INSURRECTION.*"[49] Austin represented the opinion that slavery was a permanent and ineradicable evil; any attempt to eliminate it simply meant additional evil— moral, social, and political. According to Samuel May, Channing's pamphlet found an audience among people who would not give ear to Garrison. Channing's exposé, he said, aroused Southern slaveholders and their Northern partisans to such anger that they regarded its author as a more dangerous opponent than Garrison.[50]

Throughout the next seven years, as has already been indicated, Channing expressed his views about slavery in several major public pronouncements. But his essays on *The Duty of the Free States, A Letter to Henry Clay, Remarks on the Slavery Question, Emancipation,* and the Lenox Address do not change the essence of his message; they only add emphasis to his fundamental conviction that the slave must be freed because he is designed by his Creator to enjoy the same blessings and freedom as any other human being.

Channing's life closed before the issue of slavery was joined with the political and economic problems that eventually led to civil war, but the part he played in the antislavery movement found echoes in the Emancipation Proclamation that signaled the end of legal slavery twenty years after his death. Even before the question of slavery involved him, he had shown his distaste for controversy. Yet he had never shrunk from it when great principles were involved. Men like William Lloyd Garrison were always at their best in a good fight, but not Channing. He loved peace and tranquility, but no man ever possessed greater moral courage. Once he had determined the path of justice, he never failed to follow it. Having sacrificed his own career "to turn the crank of an opinion mill," John Greenleaf Whittier could testify from experience to Channing's contribution. He wrote William Francis, Channing's son: "As to the matter of courage and self-sacrifice very few of us have evinced so much of both as thy father. He threw upon the altar the proudest reputation, in letters and theology, of his day. With the single exception of Lydia Maria Child, I know of no one who made a greater sacrifice than thy father."[51]

CHAPTER 5

The Man of Letters

PREACHING was "the great action" of Channing's life; and conversation was "the ordinary action," according to his friend Orville Dewey.[1] Certainly Channing never considered himself a writer, for he wrote Joanna Baillie: "I have been an author by accident, not by profession or of set purpose." He also continually deprecated the efforts of friends and correspondents to play up his literary accomplishments. To be sure, the truths in his writings were "infinitely important," but he was ever conscious "of having done no justice to them."[2]

Regardless of what he might think of himself as an author, he had definite opinions about other writers and about literature in general. At Harvard and during the months of study at Richmond, he had cultivated a catholic taste for literature that leaned more to the ethical than the intellectual. Books for pleasure were "worth more than all the luxuries on earth";[3] but they served best to help man interpret what he saw and experienced. "The grand volumes, of which all our books are transcripts . . . nature, revelation, the human soul, and human life, are," he said, "freely unfolded to every eye. . . . To open and fix our eyes upon what passes without and within us, is the most fruitful study."[4]

I Literary Criticism and Influences

Shakespeare and Milton were the first giants to appear on his literary horizon; but later on, their lengthening shadows were blended with the clearer silhouettes of contemporaries like Wordsworth, Coleridge, and Carlyle. In his serious reading he concentrated upon authors who exalted man's moral and intellectual powers; and he relegated to secondary importance writers like Horace Walpole, who amused him in spite of offending his moral sentiments.[5] Thus, he ranked Milton in the order of "seraphs," while Dr. Johnson was, by comparison, earth-bound.[6] Among contemporary English poets, he gave first places to Wordsworth, "the poet of humanity," and to Coleridge to whom he owed "more than to the mind of any philosophic thinker."[7] He was taken in by the Byronic pose, however, and concluded that Lord Byron lacked "depth of thought," although he did concede that Byron's letters gave a clearer view of his intellect than his poems.[8] Shelley he saw as "a seraph gone astray, who needed friends that he never found in this world"[9]—a criticism anticipating Matthew Arnold's "ineffectual angel." Among lesser poetic worthies, he found room to praise Felicia Hemans, though at times she depressed him; and his letters to Joanna Baillie, a Scottish poet and dramatist and the friend of Walter Scott, offered criticism and encouragement.

In the realm of fiction, Channing applied his moralistic criticism even more rigorously than in poetry. Sometimes his tone is so stern and reprimanding that one is likely to question where his well-known tolerance has disappeared. An example is his stricture on Godwin, whom he had read over a period of many years: "There are some errors which show such a strange obliquity of intellect as to destroy my confidence in the judgment of those who adopt them. Godwin does not believe in a God, and such a mind must be as unsound as one which should not believe in the existence of the sun."[10] Still he was by no means immune to the appeal of an imaginative story even if its author did not measure up to his personal standard of morality. He once confessed to creating himself imaginary romances in which the heroes sound suspiciously like those made famous in time to come by Horatio Alger. But honesty compelled him to admit possible harm might come to the unwary reader who would remain satisfied with his own imperfect condition because of imaginative sympathy with the idealized existence of the heroes of romance.[11]

In his reading and criticism of contemporary novelists,

Channing showed everywhere his preference for writers who were faithful to his concepts of human nature. Thus Bulwer's *The Last Days of Pompeii* failed to impress him because of a lack of life and reality in the major characters.[12] He acknowledged his debt to Scott for many pleasurable moments but could not place him among the greatest authors:

> He was anything but a philosopher. But in *extent* of observation, in the quick perception of the endless varieties of human character, in the discovery of their signs and manifestations, and in the inventive and graphic power by which he embodies them . . . where will you find his equal?[13]

Though not Scott's equal in inventiveness and hardly comparable in use of language, Henry Taylor in his *Philip Van Artevelde* impressed Channing with the insight into real people and human greatness that he found lacking in Scott, who never rose above "the ideal of a man of the world."[14] Goethe, too, merited reserved praise from Channing and was no match for Schiller because "he did not conceive the essential divinity of human nature." Though it took an entire winter, Channing and Elizabeth Peabody managed to struggle through *Wilhelm Meister* with time out at frequent intervals to read the "more enlivening" sketches of Mary Mitford.[15]

Like Milton, Channing believed there was a high correlation between what one was as a person and how one wrote. So he filled his library with the best authors (*morally* best) in order to build up a reverence for virtue and to strengthen himself in his battle against human imperfection. And like Milton again, he wanted to write a great work that would demonstrate man's potential for freedom and perfection.

Apparently the idea for such a work came early in his career as a minister although he did not mention it until after his return from England in 1823. Then scattered references to it, increasing in frequency of appearance as time went on, recur in his private papers and in his correspondence. Apparently it was to have been an examination of human nature "to determine its central law, and the end for which all religious and political institutions should be established."[16]

To accomplish his lofty purpose, Channing had planned a work consisting of three parts: the first to deal with man; the second, with God; and the third, with the duties resulting from man's relationship to God. The eight chapters of the first part which were composed—a rather pitiful fragment of accomplishment to represent the plans and aspirations of nearly an entire lifetime—are only first sketches; and they lack clarity and organization. Various threads of influence are discernible; but there is no pattern to indicate a rationale behind the material that had been collected.

The general background of the fragment is eighteenth century. It begins in true Lockean fashion with a discussion of sensation; but it follows up the Lockean lead with ideas borrowed from the Scotch School which came after Locke. Sensations are described as "occasions" rather than "causes" of intellectual activity, and the mind is cited as furnishing the universe from its own store instead of deriving its riches from it.[17]

The idealism of the piece is incontestable, but Channing's eclectic method makes identification of specific sources virtually impossible. He had drawn from Plato and Price, Wordsworth and Coleridge, Cousin and Jouffroy, Kant and Carlyle; but a lack of critical acumen prevented his welding these materials into a coherent system. Gifted with the mind of neither an Edwards nor a Hume, he was as incapable of erecting a logical edifice like the *Freedom of the Will* or the *Treatise of Human Nature* as he was of arguing in behalf of human depravity and a blood atonement. Channing's talent was not to devise systems of logic but to drive home—through the dense barriers of stale custom and habit and in spite of human inertia—a few great ideas by force of example and by constant reiteration in conversation, sermon, and pamphlet.

Naturally Channing was disappointed by his lack of progress on his *magnum opus,* but he was accustomed to temporizing with circumstances. He counted his time well spent because he could remember that his sermons and discourses had been enriched by his study. Besides he had written much more on account of it. Writing, he believed, was one of the great means of giving precision, clearness, consistency, and energy to thought; and for a long time he had attempted to sharpen his powers of concentration by increasing his efforts in composition. "One of the great laws of our nature, and a law singularly important to social beings," he said, "is, that the intellect enlarges and strengthens itself by expressing worthily its best views. . . . Superior minds are formed, not merely by solitary thought, but almost as much by communication."[18]

In his emphasis upon clarity and precision and upon the power of the written word to improve the mind, Channing followed in the steps of those eighteenth-century arbiters of taste, Lord Kames and Hugh Blair, both of whom he had studied at Harvard and whom his brother, Edward Tyrell, taught, along with Archibald Alison and Thomas Brown of the Scotch School, to Harvard undergraduates like Emerson, Holmes, and Thoreau. Moreover, when Dr. Channing declared that "the laborious distribution of a great subject, so as to assign to each part or topic its just position and due proportion, is singularly fitted to give compass and persevering force of thought,"[19] he was not only following the pattern of discourse established in New England by the early Puritan ministers but also proving himself a good disciple of Addison by using the standard idiom of neoclassic decorum. Aesthetically, he looked both backward and forward; he acknowledged as late as 1837 his humility before "the spontaneous graces" of Addison and Goldsmith, yet he wrote almost simultaneously in his projected treatise that beauty was in the mind, as the Scotch School argued, and not in the objects perceived by the mind.[20]

Up to the very close of his writing career, therefore, Channing was an exponent of eighteenth-century methods of writing as well as of the more mechanical and technical aspects of its rules on style. Perspicuity, force, and precision are spelled out in his sermons and critical articles; and his purism in language is demonstrated by the avidity with which he seized upon neologisms in the letters of his correspondents. That he became a writer by accident, as Renan charged, is partially true, but that none of his works "exhibits the least pretension to art or style" is completely false.[21] To the larger and less cut-and-dried features of style he devoted much attention; and he seldom neglected, especially in his ordination sermons, to emphasize the importance of developing a personal style in both written and spoken communication. It was, he believed, the primary factor in determining the creative power of a writer; and it depended very little upon the structure of sentences and size of vocabulary, but chiefly upon the mind of the person writing. He was asserting, therefore, the power of the mind (or soul) to invigorate art. By so doing, he was putting aside the cold and mechanical standards of Kames and Blair for the warm and organic principles of the romantics. He was still a "judicious" critic of literature; but his moralism was rather the dynamic doctrine of Wordsworth and Coleridge than the negative didacticism of Addison and Steele. Insofar as he emphasized the spiritual relationship between man and nature, he was giving expression to the idealism of his age in much the same way as the English romantics.

II *Estimates of Channing*

Channing's dualism in attitude accounted for the varying estimates of his work both at home and abroad. Philosophically like Wordsworth, Coleridge, and Carlyle, he was also received by the English quarterly reviewers as one of themselves. During the period between his return from England and the seven or eight years following his death, English critics ranked him next to Irving and Cooper. This opinion aroused criticism in America not because of Channing's eminence but because writers like William Cullen Bryant and Fitz-Greene Halleck had been overlooked.[22] In general, his reputation at home ranged from the conservative judgments of Emerson to the encomiums of some of his parishioners.[23] Even during the years when his name was an abomination to Southern slaveholders, the same lips that excoriated him paid tribute to his skill as an author.

There were several good reasons for his recognition by English as well as American critics—and they were not due primarily to his reputation as a leading Unitarian apologist. His critical essays on Milton and Napoleon were the first examples in America of the kind of judicial criticism that made the *Edinburgh Review* famous,[24] and his remarks on *The Importance and Means of a National Literature* (1830) anticipated the independence of mind proclaimed by Emerson in *The American Scholar* (1837). Far from being just an exposition of controversial religious dogma, his writing, as Emerson realized, was "almost a history of the times." And his religious idealism, which may seem outmoded today, was just what the more enlightened people of his age wanted to hear. Vice, poverty, and crime, he told them, were strange garb for the sons of God; and the words sounded very convincing when he uttered them. Self-culture seemed a natural program in the expansive years following the revolutionary successes in America and France, and there was no more forceful or convincing expositor of the doctrine than he in the America of the twenties and thirties.

For his English readers and his American audience as well, he provided a link between Coleridge and Carlyle and Ruskin. The spirituality of the former echoed in his journal and public utterances, while his articles on Milton, Napoleon, and Fénelon preached the doctrine of heroism that Carlyle later elaborated. Finally, the dignity of manual labor—which was to be emphasized by Carlyle, Ruskin, and William Morris—found expression a generation earlier in his lectures on *Self-Culture, The Elevation of the Laboring Classes,* and *The Present Age.*

Up to the time of his visits to London and other metropolitan centers of England in 1823, his reputation as a Unitarian leader had not penetrated very far into the British Isles. At home he was known only by his articles on the Unitarian controversy and by a few sermons, the most important of which was the address at Sparks' ordination in Baltimore. After his return to America, however, his tracts and sermons were reprinted regularly in Liverpool, Manchester, Bristol, Glasgow, and London; and they received frequent notice in the religious journals. When his *Remarks on the Character and Writings of John Milton* was published in London in 1826, not much notice was taken of it until it ran into a second edition in the year of the pamphlet republication of his *Analysis of the Life and Character of Napoleon Bonaparte* (1828).[25] By the time his article on Fénelon appeared the following year, his literary reputation was ready to keep pace in both America and London with his theological one; and the reprinting in England of *The Importance and Means of a National Literature* was a matter of course. From 1830 until his death, his works were issued almost simultaneously on both sides of the Atlantic.

The London *Monthly Magazine* was the first to acknowledge the worth of the critical essays about Milton and Napoleon and found little to criticize in them except the strictures on Dr. Johnson in the *Milton*.[26] *The Westminster Review* thought the Bonaparte article excellent, exclaiming that "Dr. Channing was the first man, whose bold and mighty breathings dissipated the delusive mist of fame which hung round the brow of Napoleon."[27]

William Hazlitt disagreed sharply with this opinion. The first two volumes of his *Life of Napoleon Bonaparte* had just been published, and there were two volumes to come. Scott's *Life of Napoleon* had anticipated his by a year, a fact which did not improve his good nature; and now Channing's essay, which unsparingly attacked one of Hazlitt's idols, appeared. Furthermore, Channing had publicly opposed the English brand of Unitarianism of which Hazlitt's father had been a leader. For all these reasons it is easy to see why Hazlitt's usually tart pen was dipped in gall when he criticized the American writer.

After Channing's first essay on Napoleon had been reprinted in London at least four times and his second at least twice, Hazlitt wrote a "Review of *Sermons and Tracts*, by W. E. Channing" for the *Edinburgh Review*, in which he prefaced his criticism of Channing by some general remarks about American literature. "Of the later American writers, who besides Dr. Channing have acquired some reputation in English," says Hazlitt, "we can only recollect Mr. Washington Irving, Mr. Brown and Mr. Cooper." After grudging praise to Irving and backhanded compliments to Brown and Cooper, Hazlitt finally reached Channing:

> Dr. Channing is a great tactitian in reasoning; and reasoning has nothing to do with tactics. We do not like to see a writer constantly trying to steal a march upon opinion without having his retreat cut off—full of pretensions, and void of offense. . . . He keeps an eye on both worlds; kisses hands to the reading public all around; and does his best to stand

> well with different sects and parties. . . . We like Dr. Chan-
> ning's Sermons best; his Criticism less; his politics least of
> all. We think several of his discourses do great honour to
> himself and his profession. . . . His notice of Milton is
> elaborate and stately, but neither new nor discriminating. . . .
> This is the general feature of our author's writings; they
> cannot be called mere commonplace. . . . Dr. Channing's
> Esays on Milton and Bonaparte are both done upon the
> same false principle, of making out a case *for* or *against*. The
> one is full of commonplace eulogy, the other commonplace
> invective. They are pulpit criticisms.[28]

Regardless of how angry he might be, Hazlitt always managed to sow some wheat among the cockleburs of his criticisms. Thus, while he was grossly unfair in challenging Channing's intellectual morality, he was more than three-quarters right in calling Channing's essays "pulpit utterances" and in singling out the ethical obsession that led Channing to exalt Milton and belittle Napoleon.

However sincere Hazlitt might have been in regarding the Milton article as neither "new nor discriminating," he did scant justice to the new philosophical and religious concepts underlying Channing's criticism. In addition to defending the essential ideality of poetry, Channing had, in his description of the "serious poet," defined abstract greatness (in terms of intellectual and moral superiority) according to the most progressive tendencies of the age. "Milton's fame," he said, "rests chiefly on his poetry. . . . Of all God's gifts of intellect, he esteemed poetical genius the most transcendent. He esteemed it in himself as a kind of inspiration, and wrote his great works with something of the conscious dignity of a prophet. We agree with Milton in his estimate of poetry. It seems to us the divinest of all arts."[29] Thus, when he came to the end of his essay he used Milton as an example of the ideal "hero," although that word did not appear in his text:

> We believe that the sublime intelligence of Milton was
> imparted, not for his own sake only, but to awaken kindred
> virtue and greatness in other souls. Far from regarding him
> as standing alone and unapproachable, we believe that he
> is an illustration of what all, who are true to their nature,
> will become in the progress of their being; and we have held

him forth, not to excite an ineffectual admiration, but to
stir up our own and others' breasts to an exhilarating pursuit
of high and ever-growing attainments in intellect and virtue.[30]

Employing the same moral yardstick he used to judge
Milton, he scrutinized Napoleon's character and found him
lacking in true greatness. "But some will say," he declared,
"he was still a great man. This we mean not to deny. But
we would have it understood, that there are various kinds
of orders of greatness, and that the highest did not belong to
Bonaparte."[31] Then followed a classification which was to
echo through the social criticism of the century. First came
moral greatness, or magnanimity; second, *intellectual* greatness, or genius; and third, the greatness of *action,* or the power
of "conceiving bold and expansive plans."[32] To this final
order belonged the greatness of Napoleon.

It was really Channing's "egotism" rather than his classification of greatness that bothered Hazlitt. "Dr. Channing," he
said, "very gravely divides greatness into different sorts, and
places himself at the top among those who *talk* about things—
commanders at the bottom among those who only *do* them."[33]
It was the inevitable rejoinder addressed to those who would
teach mankind, and it betrayed the usual ignorance of the
didactic function. Emerson was much more understanding.
Years later he wrote, "I attribute much importance to two
papers of Dr. Channing, one on Milton and one on Napoleon.
. . . They were widely read, and of course immediately fruitful
in provoking emulation which lifted the state of Journalism."[34]

Channing's *Fénelon* was of a piece with his other essays,
but it received less attention than his writings about Milton
and Napoleon. It is of interest, however, because of what it
says about Channing's views of the interrelationship of religion and literature. "If we wished to impoverish a man's
intellect," he says, "we could devise few means more effectual,
than to confine him to what is called a course of theological
reading."[35] How "wonderful," he goes on, "that such a subject
[religion] should be treated so monotonously as to be pro-
verbially dull, that its professed explorers should be able to
plant their footsteps so exactly in the track of their predecessors, that the boundlessness of the field should so seldom
tempt an adventurous spirit from the beaten way. . . ."[36]

A new day was dawning for both theology and literature, Channing intimated. Since literature had lost both power and interest when it became divorced from religion and the latter had suffered stagnation because of its isolation from other areas of human experience, he suggested a union of the two was once again in order. "A beautiful literature springs from the depth and fulness of intellectual and moral life, from an energy of thought and feeling, to which nothing, as we believe, ministers so largely as enlightened religion."[37]

Channing's reputation as an American writer worthy of recognition in England was unimpaired by Hazlitt's criticism. The *Westminster* continued to be his loyal friend, reviewing in 1830 his essays on Fénelon and *Associations*, together with the *Sermons and Tracts*, which Hazlitt had scorned. "We consider Dr. Channing as an incarnation of the intellectual spirit of Christianity," its reviewer wrote. "He is the tenth Avatar of the principle of reformation; and come to complete the work. . . . America has a right to be proud of Channing; and shame would it be for the criticism of England were he to be dismissed with affected contempt."[38]

"You do not tell me what the French say about the American Channing," commented "The Lounger" in the *New Monthly Magazine*. "I am anxious to know. His works are reviewed in the proper spirit of reviewing in the last *Westminster*. It is high time that we English are willing to be the first to echo an American's praise. The fact is that when the Americans read our periodicals they suppose us hostile to them—no such thing." The writer was apparently unaware that Hazlitt had written the hypercritical article in the *Edinburgh*, for he went on to say, "The Scotch write our periodicals and it is the Scotch (the last nation in the world to do justice to a new people) who abuse them."[39]

With the essay on *National Literature* in 1830, Channing's literary reputation in England reached its peak. The *Athenaeum*, which had once lumped him in with Irving and Cooper as an imitator of his English betters, now described him as "decidedly a man of high literary attainments, of a refined taste, a discriminating judgment, with an acute, vigorous, and comprehensive mind," but objected to his style as "frequently diffuse and elaborately redundant."[40] Five years later, in

"Literature of the Nineteenth Century, America," an American writer for this same periodical credited the English for introducing Channing to the world of letters. "Even the great Channing," he said, "though always revered for his piety and eloquence, by the immediate circle of his sect, was never generally known and admired in America, as the most powerful writer of his time, until the echo came back from England." Later he continued, "The *lay* productions, on which the literary reputation of this great divine is founded, are very few; a small volume of essays comprise them all. Yet in these small limits, the hand of the master are [*sic*] so visible—the thoughts are of such broad sculpture—the language is so severely beautiful—and the truth and loftiness of the author's mind are so stamped upon every line, that, if he were not the leader of a powerful sect, and should he never write more, his fame would have pedestal enough."[41]

At home in America, Alexander H. Everett, reviewing Channing's discourse on the "Ministry for the Poor," was saying equally laudable things. Believing Channing even a better writer than Irving, he wrote, "as respects the mere form of language, we rather give the preference to the style of Dr. Channing. It is equally elegant, and a little more pure, correct and pointed that that of Mr. Irving."[42]

When a second collected edition of Channing's work was published in Glasgow in 1837, praise followed almost as a matter of course. Although a reviewer for *Fraser's Magazine* could not "acquiesce in the meagre and unhappy creed" of its author or have "any sympathy with his republican preferences, he nevertheless proclaimed him "unquestionably, the finest writer of the age." The writer, an Anglican, labeled Channing "a low Socinian" in this article but declared in another that his "reviews of character, be it intellectual or physical, are models."[43]

Not long after this enthusiastic judgment appeared, Channing had his second experience with another able but critical Englishman. This time it was Henry Peter Brougham, one of the original founders of the *Edinburgh*, who took exception to his writing. Stylistically the two men had much in common, but Channing possessed one article of faith which Brougham could not admit: he preferred fitness to lucidity. In the

Milton, he had said that "energy and richness" were much more important qualities of style than "simplicity and perspicuity"; and he had argued that a noble thought or emotion ought not to be reduced to a commonplace for the sole purpose of making it clear to inferior intelligences:

> The best style is not that which puts the reader most easily and in the shortest time in possession of a writer's naked thoughts; but that which is the truest image of a great intellect, which conveys fully and carries farthest into other souls the conception and feelings of a profound and lofty spirit. To be universally intelligible is not the highest merit. A great mind cannot, without injurious constraint, shrink itself to the grasp of common passive readers.[44]

These were sentiments to which Brougham could not assent. In words that would fit the pages of a twentieth-century periodical conducting its annual campaign against obscurity in literature, Brougham charged Channing with a "false theory" of taste. "His favorite," he declared, "is the enigmatic style, not the lucid, not the perspicuous. . . ."[45] Following this, he complained about Channing's "careless thinking and faulty diction" and identified his talent as being "of a showy and shining rather than a sterling kind. . . ."[46] The tenor of Brougham's other remarks was similar. In summary, Channing was found guilty of contaminating taste by laying down false rules of criticism and by forming his own writings on a false model of excellence.

If Brougham's criticism bore little relation to fact, Channing himself was partly to blame. He had not chosen the happiest phrasing to explain his view of the relationship between force and clarity; and, in selecting the prose of Milton as an example of "power" writing, he had not been on the safest ground. Certainly he was not describing his own style when he wrote: "We delight in long sentences, in which a great truth, instead of being broken upon into numerous periods is spread out in its full proportions, is irradiated with variety of illustration and imagery, is set forth in a splendid affluence of language and flows, like a full stream, with a majestic harmony which fills at once the air and the soul."[47] In attempting to elevate Milton's prose to a position "hardly inferior to his best poetry," he had done himself an injustice. Brougham was in a more tenable position when he declared: "Milton wrote Prose upon a False system and Poetry on a True."[48]

News of Brougham's article traveled quickly across the Atlantic. Channing was taken completely by surprise and wrote Lucy Aikin that he could see no reason for Brougham's attack. "Our paths are too distant to let us jostle one another. Then he must be conscious that his gifts, by their *kind,* to say nothing of their extent, have given him a conspicuousness before which my reputation makes little show."[49]

For the most part, Channing's admirers took no stock in Brougham's charge of false taste; but there were some in whom the "green-eyed monster" lurked, as the following quotation from a letter of Joseph Coggeshell addressed to Mrs. William Prescott, wife of a distinguished Boston judge, demonstrates:

> What do they say in Boston to the attack in the Edinburgh on the seraphic doctor—& what will Dr say himself to being classed with the Narcissus school—I am not sorry to see him combed down a little, for I do think he was mounted on rather high stilts. Since I heard of his purpose of writing a manual for the human race, I have thought it might be well for him to know, that he is not either an universal idol or an universal oracle—I am glad too that the attack is in the Edinburgh & not in the Quarterly & that it is in literary & not in religious opinions & still more that it is on the most recent of all the Dr's productions "The Character & Writings of Milton" & on the very point, for which his admirers have most commended him the beauty of his composition.[50]

There were others in America who considered Channing too big for his boots, but usually the charge was based not upon literary grounds but rather upon his "meddling" in politics or in some other area considered unsuitable for a man of the cloth. After he entered the slavery controversy, reviews of his works became so colored by his critics' personal bias that it was difficult to tell whether friendly criticism was ironic, or unfriendly attacks pure malice aforethought.

There were many reviews of Channing's work in England after the second *Edinburgh* attack, some for and some against, few altogether complimentary, but all plainly indicating that Channing was a writer who could not be ignored. Such a judgment would never have been reached had he not written acceptably according to the standards of the time and in a mode familiar to his English reviewers. Both they and he had been brought up in the same schools of thought; they had read the same textbooks; their criteria for judging were pretty much the same. Although they might not see eye to eye on details, they possessed too much in common to be long at odds with each other. As a social and literary critic, according to the day's standards, Channing possessed the background, culture, and writing skill to earn and keep a solid reputation.

By his own critical standards also he deserved to be considered among the better writers of his age. His *Remarks on A National Literature*, like Emerson's *American Scholar*, stated a creed which its author practiced by living. When he wrote his essays and sermons, he was simply trying to practice what he was always preaching. If he fell far short of the ideals that he had established for a great literature, it was only because he lacked ability—not the will—to realize them.

III *Plea for a National Literature*

When his friends read the "Remarks" in the *Christian Examiner*, they must have found it very familiar. The essay began with a broad and all-inclusive definition of literature that was the stock in trade of the day's reviewers. It was described as the expression of a nation's mind in writing, which meant that no group of gifted men should be neglected "whether devoted to the exact sciences, to mental and ethical philosophy, to history and legislation, or to fiction and poetry."[51]

After this introduction, Channing then proceeded to map out his major line of argument. A dynamic literature is needed in America, he said, because it is "among the most powerful methods of exalting the character of a nation, of forming a better race of men."[52] So far, he continued, America has done little to reflect her true nature abroad although the names of Franklin and Edwards have carried her reputation to the far corners of Europe. Because she has failed to provide "for the liberal training of the intellect, for forming great scholars, for communicating that profound knowledge, and the thirst for higher truth, which can alone originate a commanding literature,"[53] she has been unable to produce a literature worthy of her unique insights, as a democratic country, into the nature of man as a social and political being.

As a result, she has tended to rely on Europe for intellectual stimulation, largely because of the "narrow utility" of her own people which rules out "elegant literature" and thus confounds the major truth "that the idea of beauty is an indestructible principle of our nature." But America must not be simply an echo of what is "thought and written under the aristocracies beyond the ocean." Since man is the proper center of literature and since "juster and profounder views of man may be expected here, than elsewhere," said Channing, America must accept her responsibility to write his true history.

Like his predecessors Paine, Jefferson, and Freneau—and for that matter, Puritan divines and political leaders before them—Channing was a dreamer who firmly believed that America had a rendezvous with destiny not yet given to any other nation or people. His dream is embodied in the following passage:

> We should have no heart to encourage native literature, did we not hope that it would become instinct with a new spirit. We cannot admit the thought, that this country is to be only a repetition of the old world. We delight to believe that God, in the fulness of time, has brought a new continent to light, in order that the human mind should move here with a new freedom, should frame new social institutions, should explore new paths, and reap new harvests.[54]

If, then, literature was a nation's mind in writing and if it must contain "a new spirit," where were the writers to be found? Who would speak for it? Channing was only too well aware that the people at large possessed neither the knowledge nor the capacity to speak for themselves. And so he was compelled to settle for something less than a broad, representative literature. In its place should be "the action of the most gifted understandings on the community."[55] Like his younger contemporaries among the Transcendentalists, Channing was becoming more impressed by the emanations from the mind of divinity but even more skeptical of the untutored man's imaginings.

The means of producing a national literature were several: a general fostering of it wherever and whenever it might appear; the enlargement of literary institutions and the staffing of them with competent personnel; the improvement of universities and other educational institutions; and a new development of the religious principle. Channing was quick to assert, however, that these were only means and not causes, for "literature depends on individual genius, and this, though fostered, cannot be created by outward helps."[56] Finally, he suggested that Americans turn their attention to the continent and curtail their interest in things English lest they become imbued with the utilitarianism of that country.

Few American critics of the nineteenth century managed to escape the pitfall of cultural nationalism, and Channing's essay could very well have contributed to their downfall. But the respect that he himself held for man *per se* kept him from falling into the error of exalting his own national group above man in general. As he put it, "We love our country much, but mankind more."[57] True independence of mind knows no national boundaries, and he was fully aware that America could not progress in a literary vacuum any more than she could remain politically free while the rest of the world was in chains.

This essay marked his final appearance in the *Examiner* as a literary critic. He had kept his promise to the editors to help them get the magazine off to a good start; and it became, largely because of his efforts, the most important periodical of the day. His article on Milton had been the first significant piece of criticism to appear in its pages, and its campaign for an American literature had been inaugurated by his essay. Until 1829 it had an appeal that was primarily theological; but after Channing's challenge, it espoused literary criticism with a vigor and freshness that enabled it to assume a commanding position among literary journals in the years 1830 to 1835. Channing's moral idealism permeated the criticism of its editors and contributors and left its impress upon nearly every article that appeared in it during the thirties.[58]

Although he never again resorted to a periodical to express his views about literature, he had by no means said his last word about it. In 1838, while introducing the Franklin Lectures to the Boston working classes, he took the opportunity to summarize the basic creed of Self-Culture that underlay all his hopes for an improved literature, and hence for an improved race. Of all the discoveries men need to make, he told the apprentices sitting before him, the most important at this moment is the self-forming power treasured up in them. Once this is done, he went on to say, men can begin to appreciate properly the idea that "the beauty of the outward creation is intimately related to the lovely, grand, interesting attributes of the soul."[59] Literature, he concluded, is one of the most valuable means for making that relationship clear.

Three years later, he echoed the same sentiments in his oration before the Mercantile Library Company of Philadelphia. Speaking upon "The Present Age," the same topic which had been assigned to him more than forty years before in his Harvard valedictory, he identified those developments of the age which seemed to him worthiest of being encouraged. Literature was, of course, high on his list. Singling out those writers whose works seemed to express the most universal sympathy for human nature—Wordsworth, Scott, and Dickens —he paid particular attention to Wordsworth. "The great truth which pervades his poetry," he said, "is that the beautiful is not confined to the rare, the new, the distant, to scenery and modes of life open only to the few; but that it is poured forth profusely on the common earth and sky."[60]

This remark and many others like it reveal his general optimism. A true disciple of Rousseau, at least to the extent that he believed "Human nature is not a tiger which needs a constant chain," he looked with unclouded eye to the future, willing "to see some outbreak of enthusiasm, whether transcendental, philanthropic, or religious," as long as it indicated that the human spirit was not wholly engulfed in material considerations.

When the first collected edition of his writings appeared in 1841, Channing wrote a lengthy introduction for it, which constituted a kind of apologia *pro operibus suis*. In that introduction he described, in terms of quiet understatement, what he thought of his literary productions. "They have," he said, "the merit of being earnest expressions of the writer's mind, and of giving the results of quiet, long-continued thought."[61] And what he said was true, for the works were the man; and their lack of literary dress was characteristic of their author's mind. They were typical of the unstudied simplicity of his habitual expression. Repetitiousness and an occasional rhetorical flourish sometimes disturb the easy flow of thought, but these faults are attributable to his primary function of preaching. Like so many of his contemporaries—his cousin, Richard Henry Dana and his brother-in-law, Allston, to mention but two of the more obvious examples—he suffered from the lack of an intellectual milieu larger than himself. As Emerson so cogently put it, "Dr. Channing, had he found Wordsworth, Southey, Coleridge, and Lamb around him, would as easily have been severe with himself and risen a degree higher as he has stood where he is. I mean, of course, a genuine intellectual tribunal, not a literary junto of Edinburgh Wits, or dull conventions of Quarterly or Gentleman's Reviews."[62] He was with these men in spirit; but the activating principle of personal contact was lacking and he could not rise above the level which he himself had created. "The finest writer of his age," he was emphatically not; but neither was he an example of the proverb: "In the country of the blind, the one-eyed man is king."

CHAPTER 6

The Disciples

NONE OF CHANNING'S friends or acquaintances was ever allowed to forget for long that he considered the power of acting upon minds the greatest power in the world. His parishioners in Federal Street, the lawyers and politicians in the State House, the farmers and fishermen to whom he preached during his summers in Rhode Island, and the apprentices in Boston and Philadelphia heard the same message. God's first end in creation was Mind (by which Channing meant naturally moral as well as intellectual power), and the formation of Mind was the great purpose for which God had fixed the very order of nature.

I Seedtime of Intellect

Because of Channing's well-known penchant for Mind, many young New Englanders, hungering for intellectual stimulation in the twenties and thirties, were drawn into his orbit, where they soon came under the influence of his doctrine of self-culture. Though Channing never found it easy to unbend before others and though few ever penetrated to the warmth behind his habitual mask of reserve, the force of his convictions and the purity of his beliefs served to offset any coolness in his initial reception and to bind new friends to his cause. Women in particular found the combination of reserve and inner fire irresistible; and from Elizabeth Peabody, who became his personal secretary and an almost idolatrous defender, to Lucy Aikin, Joanna Baillie, Felicia Hemans, Dorothea Dix, Harriet Martineau, Lydia Child, Catherine Sedgwick, and numerous others as well, came testimony of Channing's considerable influence upon them and upon their work—social reforms of various kinds and the production of history, poetry, drama, and fiction.[1]

Among the young men who worked side by side in the 1820's with Channing at Federal Street, Samuel May, Orville Dewey, and Ezra Stiles Gannett reveal the deep impress that Channing made upon their minds and subsequent careers.[2] All three became imbued with their senior colleague's idealism and hopes for the future, and they played prominent roles in the movements of the forties. But none of them perhaps was ever so willing as Channing to look beyond the horizon of his immediate beliefs to views that might be better suited to changing times.

As early as 1817 young Waldo Emerson showed his interest in Dr. Channing; and, when it came time for him to choose a career, he selected the ministry—largely, one suspects, because of the older man's influence. He wrote his Aunt Mary Moody in 1823: "Dr. Channing is preaching sublime sermons every Sunday morning in Federal St. one of which I heard last Sunday, and which infinitely surpassed Everett's eloquence."[3] The following spring, when Emerson decided to give up teaching school to study divinity, he went to Channing to ask for direction. Channing gave him a reading list and agreed to talk over his studies from time to time, but he would not accept a permanent tutoring arrangement.[4] Just as with Emerson and Hawthorne later on, the barriers of reserve could not be broken because neither Channing nor Emerson were outgoing enough to take the initiative. But enough communication existed for Emerson to return to Harvard in 1825 to study theology, despite the warning of his aunt, whose Calvinism favored Andover and—if that were not possible—private "study under the wing of Channing which was never pruned at Cambridge."[5]

In the fall of 1826 another young man came under Channing's spell as Channing dedicated the new Divinity School at Harvard. Charles Follen, a refugee from persecution in Germany, was a bright young doctor of law, who had recently arrived in Cambridge to teach German; and his love of liberty and free minds found in Channing a congenial spirit.[6] The two became good friends, for Channing was eager to learn about German philosophy and Follen knew not only the original sources but also the translations into French of men like Benjamin Constant and Victor Cousin, whom he had met in Paris. For a time Channing even aspired to proficiency in the German language, but he was forced to surrender this ambition because of other duties.

II *Educational Interests*

But his interest in educational and philosophic movements abroad found other outlets. George Ticknor (the first Smith Professor of the French and Spanish languages at Harvard, and the man responsible for bringing Follen to Harvard)[7] and William Russell (a Scotsman, the editor and founder in 1826 of the *American Journal of Education* and an associate of Elizabeth and Mary Peabody in their Brookline school) joined Channing and several others who had been doing catechetical work at Federal Street to form "The Society of Education." Joseph Tuckerman, one of Channing's old classmates at Harvard, and Channing's brothers, Walter and Edward Tyrell, were added to the group, which expanded its discussions to include every educational level from pre-school to practical education for adults.

The importance of such an organization to Boston and its people cannot be overestimated. For it included Ticknor, whose training at Göttingen was esteemed invaluable by Jefferson in establishing his new university and who was trying himself to renovate the Harvard curriculum along European models; Jonathan Phillips, philanthropist and ardent supporter of Channing's theories of self-education; Russell, with his training in Scottish universities and his desire to spread education by the printed word; Follen, patriot and teacher, who could speak at first hand of the transcendental thinkers in Europe; Dr. Walter Channing, with his clinical training and medical experience among the sick and poor of Boston; Joseph Tuckerman, beginning a pioneer career as a social worker among the Boston underprivileged; and Edward Tyrell, professor of rhetoric and mentor of the scholars and writers of the Golden Day to come. And finally, at the head of them all, nudging and goading, was Dr. Channing himself—what a wealth of talents and experience!

In a few years Boston, Cambridge, and Concord would produce a crop of writers, reformers, and educators destined for future fame, but what proportion of their success would be owing to the guiding spirit of the master in Federal Street? Ralph Waldo Emerson's answer is as good as any, and he concluded that "we could not then spare a single word he uttered in public, not so much as the reading a lesson in Scripture, or a hymn . . . there was no great public interest, political, literary, or even economical . . . on which he did not leave some printed record of his brave and thoughtful opinion."[8]

Emerson's judgment was borne out in Bronson Alcott's first experiences with Channing. When Alcott's revolutionary ideas about how children were to be educated met with disfavor among the good conservative people of Connecticut, his birthplace, Alcott decided in the spring of 1828 to come to Boston. Samuel May had provided him with letters of introduction to William Russell and Ezra Gannett, and they in turn introduced him to Channing. On his first Sunday in Boston, Alcott listened to Channing preach on the "Dignity of the Intellect," and, as Bronson wrote afterward in his journal, what he heard was "an introductory course to immortality."[9] In the months that followed, the two men became friends. Alcott confided to his journal that he thought Channing the most original thinker in the city and added: "His mind is a remarkable one. It soars high. It leaves the region of material vision and seeks affinity with the objects and essences of spiritual forms."[10]

Wherever Alcott turned, he found evidence of Channing's influence. He visited Elizabeth Peabody's school; and she was, of course, always talking about Channing. Though Alcott thought her at first "offensively assertive," he later became an admirer. Dorothea Dix was an entirely different kind of schoolteacher. She had learned from Channing, she told Alcott, that no mind in the community must be overlooked and that all avenues of learning should be explored. She was now looking around for more useful ways to spend her energy, but the time was still distant when she would find a rich, untapped vein of suffering humanity in the mentally ill— the shadowy multitude of forgotten souls who were beyond the pale of sympathy.[11]

While Alcott was learning from others about the good Doctor, Channing was finding Alcott himself an interesting subject. On one score at least, he found Alcott wanting: Bronson was too much inclined to rely on his own intuitions and to downgrade the value of past experience. His practicality needed balancing with theory, and he had to learn that even education has its limitations. On the other hand, when they gathered in Channing's study to discuss government, art, or education, Alcott usually ended up by telling his host that he needed more practical experience. This Channing would not deny, but it was plain that he considered his role to be essentially behind the scenes rather than out in plain view. As time passed, Alcott began to have some misgivings about Boston, and he felt even "the splendid genius of Channing . . . inadequate to break through the remaining clouds of prejudice and intolerance which linger on its horizon."[12]

Clouds of intolerance undoubtedly did lower over Boston's horizon in 1832, but new winds of doctrine were also beginning to fill up its mental sky, eddy about its avenues of learning, and circulate through its temples of worship. More signs than one indicated that precedent and tradition were beginning to stifle the more spiritually-minded members of the community. The "corpse-cold" Unitarianism of Brattle Street and Harvard had lost much of the spirit with which Channing had originally inspired it, and now it no longer satisfied the hungry seekers after new truths. Most of them had been nourished on Channing's doctrines of self-trust and free inquiry.

Emerson was the first of the Boston ministers to seek a wider freedom than Unitarianism provided. Although he had served the Second Church less than three years, he knew without further trial that he could no longer conscientiously administer its simple rites. An article in *The New England Magazine* hinted broadly that his defection was owing largely to Channing's preaching,[13] and his Aunt Mary Moody, who had warned about "humanitarianism" all along, was inclined to agree. Channing himself remained unperturbed, but Ezra Gannett hastened to defend both him and Emerson.[14]

But Emerson was not the only "seeker." George Ripley was beginning to grow restive in the meeting-house on Purchase Street, although he had not progressed so far in rebellion as Emerson. Ever since his Harvard days Ripley had admired Channing. Ordained in 1826, he had begun his career under conservative auspices, but his inquisitive mind had not long remained content with the Lockean doctrines that Professor Andrews Norton had tried to impress upon him.[15] Channing had taught him instead that man's ultimate reliance must be on his own mind and the Scriptures could not contradict reason. Besides, Channing's system provided room for intuition, and intuition (whatever Dr. Norton thought of it) was an important channel of truth.

When Ripley preached his sermon "Jesus Christ the same Yesterday, To-Day and Forever," it caused no alarm among his parishioners, nor were eyebrows raised when James Walker's tract, "The Philosophy of Man's Spiritual Nature in regard to the Foundations of Faith," appeared at approximately the same time. Yet Ripley's discourse contained the substance of Theodore Parker's Boston Sermon on the "Transient and Permanent in Christianity"; and Walker's pamphlet, published by the Unitarian Association, was an exposition of transcendentalism. Perhaps the custodians of "revealed" truth had momentarily relaxed their vigilance; whatever the cause, Channing was all for encouraging men like Alcott, Ripley, and Walker, and—yes, even the unpredictable Orestes Brownson.

Brownson was convalescing from the effects of an excursion into the infidelity of Fanny Wright when a friend read him Channing's "Likeness to God." Channing's affirmation of the potential divinity in man, which Brownson later called the most remarkable utterance "since the Sermon on the Mount,"[16] cured Brownson's doubts and converted him to Unitarianism, which he considered closer to Christianity than any other denomination.[17] When his magazine, *The Philanthropist*, failed, he moved as close to Boston as he could. From his church in Walpole, New Hampshire, he began to contribute articles about French philosophy and about Christian social progress to the *Christian Register* and the *Examiner*. His contacts with these magazines brought him frequently to Boston, where he soon met Channing and Ripley.

Channing did not warm to Brownson when they first met, but he wrote him shortly afterward that he approved of his treating Christianity as a principle of reform.[18] Soon they were exchanging pulpits, and it was not long before Ripley suggested that Brownson come to Boston to establish a church for people "who are disgusted with Orthodoxy and insensible to Liberal Christianity in any of the modes, in which it is now presented. . . ."[19] The voice was Ripley's but the words were Channing's.

For years Channing had been thinking of a "Church of the Future," and one of the means he had considered to bring it about was to preach the gospel to the workingmen of Boston, who were largely "unchurched" because of artificial class distinctions. These people needed someone who could speak their own language and understand their needs; Brownson's experience with the Workingman's Party seemed to make him an ideal candidate.[20] The idea appealed to Brownson, and he moved to Chelsea in 1836 and began to hold independent meetings in Boston.

A gain on one front, however, was sometimes offset by loss on another. By this time Alcott had become disenchanted with his old friend to the extent that he could call Emerson "superior to Channing."[21] The immediate cause of his reaction was Channing's reservations about his methods in the Temple School, which Channing had helped him to start. Channing had discussed his objections to Alcott's mental self-analysis with him and with Elizabeth Peabody, but Alcott remained unconvinced that analysis could endanger the spiritual development of the children in his care. Alcott's trouble, Channing decided, was that he confused human nature with God's.[22] His *Record of Conversations on the Gospels* proved Channing's judgment to be correct, but Channing could not agree with Andrews Norton that the "*Record* was one-third absurd, one-third blasphemous, and one-third obscene."

If Channing found it impossible to accept the main thesis of Alcott's *Record,* he was rewarded by a more palatable form of idealism in Carlyle's *Sartor Resartus,* which he secured from

Emerson in early March, 1835. As Emerson wrote Carlyle with undisguised admiration for Channing's interest in the newest form of infidelity,[23] ". . . please love his catholicism, that at his age can relish the *Sartor,* born and inveterated as he is in the old books."[24] Carlyle himself was pleased though somewhat surprised that Channing's tolerance might extend to him. He replied to Emerson: "His own faithful, long-continued striving toward what is Best, I knew and honored; that he will let me go my own way thitherward, with a God-speed from him, is surely a new honor to us both."[25] Judging by this exchange, both Emerson and Carlyle had failed, until this moment, to gauge the calibre of Channing's response to new directions in thought.

True, he was no transcendentalist. Nor would he ever become one, because, as he had cautioned even in that most transcendental of his utterances, "Likeness to God," he saw too much divinity in the normal operations of human nature to wish to urge on it a forced virtue. "To grow in the likeness of God," he warned, "we need not cease to be men."[26] Not for him, therefore, the moment of ecstasy that would bring Emerson to write: "I become a transparent eyeball; I am nothing; I see all; the currents of the Universal Being circulate through me; I am part or parcel of God." Still he would never gainsay Emerson's right to think such thoughts. As a matter of fact, he expected Emerson to do for him what Carlyle was so successful in doing—i.e., quicken his thoughts—and he followed intently the course of Emerson's career because, as he said, "Mr. Emerson seems to be gifted to speak to an audience which is not addressed by the rest of us."[27]

III *Transcendentalism*

Yet his own work must go on, and he had to do it in his own way. Shortly before the appearance of Emerson's *Nature,* he had suggested to George Ripley that he and a few others ought to found a society for "mutual inquiry." Ripley thought the suggestion excellent and proposed to have a meeting soon. The following September, a group composed of Alcott, Emerson, Frederick Hedge, Convers Francis, Brownson, and James

Freeman Clarke met at Ripley's home and the Symposium, or Transcendental Club, as it was later named, was born.[28] Channing attended the Club only once, but he did continue to participate as actively as ever in another group that met in Jonathan Phillips' rooms at the Tremont House.[29] The Friends, as the group was called, included, besides Channing, Phillips, and Follen, three members of the Trancendental Club, Alcott, Hedge, and Ripley. Among them, these men could report on almost any aspect of the community one might name or, at least, would want to name.

By now Brownson's "Society for Christian Union and Progress" was well under way with a program consisting of three simple articles: intellectual liberty, social progress, and a more spiritual morality than that which animated the ministers who took care not to offend State Street. Channing's conservative friends viewed the undertaking as radical, but Channing wrote Elizabeth Peabody that he preferred Brownson's "morbidly sensitive vision to prevalent evils, to the stoneblindness of the multitudes who condemn him."[30] More practically, he gave freely of his money as well as his counsel.

The Society did not continue to justify his complete confidence, however. Brownson was inclined to default on inner reform now and again and to seek for purely social solutions to the problems of the working class. When the Bank Panic of 1837 opened Brownson's eyes to the havoc of economic depression, he told Channing he would have to change his methods. He could not ask *hungry* people to put their trust in religion and education. Prayer would not call down manna from heaven, and State Street did not choose to feed those in the bread lines though it very easily could. The only solution lay in political action, and the only party that seemed likely to be helpful was the Democratic one. He would support it.

Channing was disappointed but not discouraged. He found a replacement for Brownson in his favorite nephew, William Henry Channing, who had recently returned from abroad with some new ideas. In Paris Henry had learned Baron de Gerando's *Le Visiteur du Pauvre* by heart, and he had studied various European charitable organizations.[31] Upon his reunion with his uncle, Henry had so enthusiastically poured forth his ideas about starting a ministry for the poor in New York that Channing agreed to back his efforts to combine a ministry among the underprivileged with a program of religious instruction for workingmen.

The new undertaking proved short-lived. Henry found an entrenched orthodoxy and the economic problems resulting from the Panic too much to overcome. He returned to Boston, his ardor somewhat dimmed, and shortly afterward set out to join James Freeman Clarke in Cincinnati. Under his direction, but in the spirit of Dr. Channing, *The Western Messenger* was reorganized to preach not only self-culture but a gospel of social improvement.[32] Transcendentalism on the frontier was in the way of being transformed into a reforming creed.[33]

At home education continued to be of prime importance. For some five years Channing with interest had watched Horace Mann's career in the Massachusetts legislature. When Mann threw aside his promising political career to become secretary of the newly organized Massachusetts Board of Education, Channing wrote him, exclaiming, "You could not find a nobler station. You must allow me to labor under you according to my opportunities. If at any time I can aid you, you must let me know."[34] Mann took up his offer and soon invited him to attend an educational convention in Taunton. Accepting, Channing gave a lengthy extemporaneous speech about the value of common school education that so pleased Mann he was eager to have him repeat the performance on other occasions. Channing's health limited him to moral support largely; but even that was important and Mann frequently called upon him for advice.[35]

Channing's time was also beginning to be taken up by long discussions with another new acquaintance, the Reverend Theodore Parker, youthful pastor of the church in Roxbury. They spent whole afternoons together discussing such matters as conscience, miracles, and materialism. Parker was not one to stand in awe of any man, and he never backed down when he and Channing disagreed. Such occasions were frequent because Parker's transcendentalism had taken him far away from the views of Christ and revelation that Channing held. For Parker intuition provided the only infallible guide, and the character of Christ was a model to which any man might hope to aspire.

When Channing introduced Parker to the Friends, he found that the newcomer fitted easily into the group. He always enjoyed the evenings at the Tremont himself because they afforded him an opportunity to play the role of Socrates among people who were capable of responding to that approach. He liked to get Ripley or Alcott talking about progress because it was a subject of which no one ever seemed to tire and one that produced a seemingly endless line of new inquiry. The Friends agreed generally that society was moving, but they were less confident that men themselves were any more altruistic than in days past.[36]

Sometimes, instead of dealing with such broad subjects as progress, the group attacked more specific topics. After Emerson's address at the Harvard Divinity School, they discussed not only what he had said but whether Emerson was a Christian or a Pantheist. Parker, of course, defended Emerson against a charge that seemed to him too vague to have any validity. Pantheism meant that God was only an idea of man's mind, and he could not accept such a definition of Emerson's views. Although Channing objected to the ambiguity of some of Emerson's language, he thought Emerson's ideas were essentially the same as his own. Certainly Emerson had spoken truly when he asserted that the age of inspiration was not past and the Bible not closed. Had he not himself at the opening of the Divinity School dedicated its halls to free inquiry and had not Emerson simply followed his advice to future ministers "to utter, in their own manly tones, what their own free investigation and deep conviction urge them to preach as the truth of God"?[37]

Not long after this discussion, rumor spread that Channing had criticized Emerson for preaching against Christianity in a school dedicated to Christian principles. Elizabeth Peabody went to Channing to ask for clarification because it upset her to think that her two favorites were at odds. Channing assured her that his remarks had been misconstrued and that he had not passed judgment on Emerson. He had merely said hypothetically that it would have been more courteous for Emerson to speak elsewhere if he had intended to deny Christianity.[38]

Channing then went on to refer to the recent sermon Henry Ware, Jr., his old friend and Emerson's former colleague, had preached in an effort to exonerate the teachers and students of the Divinity School from any blame for Emerson's "transcendental" heresy; and he said he thought that Ware, in attempting to answer Emerson, was only fighting a shadow. Ware, he added, had charged Emerson with denying the personality of God, but he himself had not so understood Mr. Emerson. The significant thing to remember, he concluded, was that "Mr. Emerson expressly says, and makes a great point of it, that God is *alive* not *dead*, and would have the gospel narrative to make its own impression of an indwelling life, like the growing grass."[39]

Channing believed that Emerson was a great moral and Christian teacher, and he admired him for the purity and benevolence of his personal life. Those critics who abuse Emerson, he told Elizabeth Peabody, lack "a tittle of the moral earnestness which makes him a most powerful person." Similarly, when he heard of attempts to squelch Parker because of his South Boston sermon, he wrote that he wished him "to preach what he thoroughly believes and feels."[40]

Parker's "Discourse on the Transient and Permanent in Christianity," which he had preached on May 19, 1841, at the ordination of Charles Shackford in the South Boston Church, raised a storm more violent perhaps than any of Channing's sermons ever had. According to Parker's own report, his fellow ministers called him "unbeliever," "infidel," and "atheist"; and one more vindictive than the rest demanded that he be tried, convicted, and sentenced to three years in the state prison for blasphemy.[41] There is no accounting today for emotional currents that ran dry a century ago; but from the perspective of the present, Parker's "permanent" Christianity was the logical extension of Channing's earlier revolution against entrenched orthodoxy. Channing himself knew how right Parker was in saying, "The heresy of one age is the orthodox belief and 'only infallible rule' of the next," for he had lived to see his own heterodoxy become "every man's doxy" in the late 1830's.

Still he had to wince somewhat at Parker's determination to drive intuition to its logically inevitable conclusion that a man could shove aside as "transient" all aspects of "theological" doctrine. The great idea of Parker's discourse—the immutableness of Christian truth—he responded to entirely; but Parker's failure to express belief in Christian miracles could only mean that his silence stood for a rejection of them—and, therefore, of Christ himself.[42] But Channing was one of the few among Parker's friends who did not desert him. While such Unitarian pillars as Francis Parkman, Ezra Gannett, and Nathaniel Frothingham—even Convers Francis, Parker's oldest friend in Boston—stood aloof, Channing cried out, "Let the full heart pour itself forth."[43]

He could not agree, however, with all the ideas that filled the intellectual atmosphere of the late '30's and early '40's. He followed Margaret Fuller's "Conversations" about genius, beauty, and art with interest, both because of what Margaret had to say and also because he was partially responsible for urging her to the enterprise.[44] If, as Emerson suggested to Margaret,[45] they approached Channing to draft a Declaration of Independence for their new magazine, he was unable to oblige, because Emerson himself finally wrote the introduction. When the first numbers of the *Dial* appeared, Channing was unimpressed; but so were Emerson and Carlyle. His heart went out to Alcott, who was trying to combine high thinking and plain living as a day laborer, but his sympathy fell short of Alcott's "Orphic Sayings." He wrote Elizabeth Peabody, "I do not care much for Orpheus in the 'Dial,'—his flights there amuse rather than edify me,—but Orpheus at the plough is after my own heart."[46]

Though his sympathies lay with their decisions, Channing felt sad to see the young men leaving Unitarianism. First Emerson had departed, then Parker had been practically ostracized, and now George Ripley had said farewell to his congregation. Ripley's resignation came as no surprise because Channing had known for some time that George had no heart for the philosophy of the majority of Unitarians. After the clash between Ripley and Andrews Norton over the latter's address on "The Latest Form of Infidelity" two years before, Channing had foreseen that Ripley would soon seek a freer climate of opinion.[47]

He could not blame Emerson and Parker and Ripley for blazing new trails. Unitarianism had begun as a protest and had pledged itself to progress; now it was more interested in holding fast. Perhaps all reforming bodies were subject to some law of inertia. Of one thing he was certain: "they become conservative, and out of them must spring new reformers, to be persecuted generally by the old."[48] Although he had grown increasingly dubious about associations and was ever searching for ways to get aid from society "without taking its yoke,"[49] he was attracted to several cooperative experiments just getting under way. Ripley would never have undertaken his Brook Farm Institute had Channing not encouraged him;[50] and Adin Ballou, the founder of Hopedale, received his full moral support. He wrote Ballou that he had "for a long time dreamed of an association, in which the members, instead of preying on one another . . . should live together as brothers, seeking one another's elevation and spiritual growth." At the same time he foresaw the danger "of losing in such establishments individuality, animation, force, and enlargement of mind."[51]

He sympathized with Brownson's feelings for the underprivileged, but he had little patience with his essay on "The Laboring Classes."[52] Believing that Brownson greatly exaggerated the workingmen's hardships, he wrote: "We all have a hard battle to fight. To me the matter of complaint is, not that the laboring class wants physical comforts,—though I wish these to be earned by *fewer hours* of labor,—but that they live only for their physical nature; that no better justice is done to their souls. . . ."[53] Brownson's remedies for social inequalities, he thought absurd. It was pure foolishness to talk of abolishing the law of inheritance and dividing up the estates of the dead. An equal distribution of the world's property would solve no problems! "No good can come but from the spread of intellectual and moral power among all classes, and the union of all by a spirit of brotherhood."[54]

Later, however, when Brownson sent him his letter on "The Mediatorial Life of Jesus," he congratulated him but warned,

"Some passages of your letter would lead an incautious reader
to think you a thorough-going Universalist and as asserting
the actual appropriation of the life of Christ to the whole
human race, past and present, will they or nill they."[55] Then,
wishing to show his confidence in Brownson, he added, "Let
us see you at the head of a really earnest and vital society of
your own. God made you for something more than to scatter
random shot, although these shot may sometimes be grand
ideas and may hit old errors between wind and water."[56]

To most Bostonians, James Freeman Clarke's plan to establish a Free Church whose support would be voluntary
and which would admit to membership any sincere believer
regardless of his denomination was a daring innovation, but
Channing was delighted with the prospect. He consulted
frequently with Clarke about ways and means and encouraged
his parishioners and family to join the new society. According
to Clarke, after Channing approved of the plan of operations
for the "Church of the Disciples," he warned "that the danger
would be a tendency to conform to the old established way,
as the mass exerted a great power of attraction. He said again,
emphatically, that we must be more afraid of formality than
of eccentricity."[57] The advice was characteristic, for Channing
was never more aware of the palsying weight of conformity
than in these years when he looked to a new revolution to
change the settled order of things.

He had never seen a stranger assortment of human beings
than the group that Edmund Quincy and Bronson Alcott
assembled in Chardon Street for the reformers convention, but
still he expected more from the cultivation of such soil than
from the tillage among the respectables of Beacon Street.[58]
"Nothing," he was wont to say, "terrifies me in these wildest
movements. What has for years terrified and discouraged me
is *apathy*."[59] Conversely, nothing pleased him or gave him
greater hope than to hear a young man like George Bancroft
say, "I should be proud to be even the humblest of your
fellow workers,"[60] and then to observe the unfolding of a
career exhibiting his own theories of intellectual and personal
liberty.

Thus, when his own career was nearing its close, and the
transcendentalists were building in George Ripley's words,

a "reform upon his reform," Channing seldom refused approval of their efforts. Theirs were not often his ways, nor could he accept the assumption of some irresponsibles among them who mistook their "individualities for the Transcendent."[61] Too many of them failed to see the distinction Emerson had been careful to draw between the divinity in man and Divinity itself in his poems "The Problem" and "The Sphinx." They were in danger of falling into a kind of "ego-theism," and only a true understanding of Jesus Christ could effect a cure.[62] Transcendentalism would never spread its views successfully if it cut itself off from Christianity—of that Channing was certain. Still he believed in the purity of motive of those who were concerned with the new movement, and he hoped for the best.[63]

In the person of Emerson, Channing recognized a man worthy of the future's trust. His own idea of man's greatness, which derived from his emphasis upon self-reliance and self-culture, and his dreams of a nation flourishing in the arts and manifesting devotion to all forms of liberty had all been taken over by Emerson as a part of his belief in the evolutionary spiral of progress. As for Emerson, recognition of his indebtedness to Channing changed but little over a quarter of a century. True, there were times when he criticized Channing's "tameness" and resistance to other voices; but, when all was said and done, who was there to take his place? As he told Elizabeth Peabody, "In our wantonness we often flaunt Dr. Channing, and say he is getting old; but as soon as he is ill we remember he is our Bishop, and we have not done with him yet."[64]

CHAPTER 7

The Liberal Legacy

DURING HIS LIFETIME Channing enjoyed a reputation at home that few of his contemporaries could match; abroad, from the thirties on through mid-century, he was probably more influential than any other American religious thinker. In Britain he had an enthusiastic circle of acquaintances and correspondents made up of people in religion, politics, and the arts who read his works avidly and then acted as willing apostles to spread his gospel of social regeneration, self-reliance, and self-culture. Beyond the British Isles, Channing's reputation extended to France, Italy, and Germany, where leaders of intellectual thought welcomed his ideas and incorporated them into their own writings.

From the time that he entered the lists against religious orthodoxy until he delivered his final address in the cause of antislavery, Channing occupied a preeminent place among Boston leaders. His name was synonymous with religious liberalism; and men and women from various walks of life sought his advice on questions ranging from personal matters to those of national, social, political, and literary import. When he died, the bells of every Boston church tolled the news—and those of the Roman Catholic Cathedral resounded with the rest; for his friends were to be found in every faith.

I *Influence in England and on the Continent*

In England the record of Channing's influence throughout the last quarter of his career can easily be traced in the Aikin correspondence. Although the strictures of Englishmen like William Hazlitt and Lord Brougham were not entirely undeserved, they represent a minority opinion among a chorus of widespread approval. Queen Victoria, who read his lectures and sermons, commissioned Lord Holland, the baron of Holland House, to express her gratitude to Channing.[1] When Charles Dickens published his *American Notes* (1842), he praised Channing's "high abilities and character" and expressed his admiration "for the bold philanthropy with which he has ever opposed himself to that most hideous blot and foul disgrace—Slavery."[2]

As early as 1836 George Bancroft introduced Channing's writings into Germany. In the 1840's and 1850's, as indicated by a number of translations and commentaries, interest in Channing's work ran high. Baron von Bunsen listed Channing among such company as Luther, Calvin, Böhme, and Schleiermacher in his *Gott in der Geschichte* (1858), but a more interesting example of his vogue in Germany occurred fifteen years earlier. In his *Der gebildete Bürger*, Berthold Auerbach incorporated a translation of Channing's entire essay about self-culture, which seems to have exerted considerable influence on Auerbach's social philosophy and on his later *Dorfgeschichten* and novels.[3]

During his lifetime Channing carried on a correspondence with Frenchmen like Baron de Gérando and Chateaubriand, although never on the extensive scale that he wrote to his friends in England. In 1838 his *Remarks on National Literature* was translated into French and widely read. French approval after his death is marked by several studies, among which Ernest Renan's essay in *Etudes d'histoire religieuse* (1862) stands out as a tribute to Channing's impact on the French people despite the author's disparagement of Channing's intellectual capacity. Earlier, Laboulaye gave unqualified approval in the *Journal des débats* (1852). In 1876 French appreciation reached a climax in René La Vollée's laudatory study, *Channing, sa Vie et sa Doctrine*, which was awarded high honors by the French Academy of Moral and Political Science.

In Spain, Switzerland, Hungary, and Italy, Channing was translated and his reputation extended by word of mouth among those who found his doctrine of self-improvement to their liking. Queen Marguerite of Italy was a strong admirer, and Charles Sismondi in Switzerland corresponded faithfully for a number of years.

II *The American Reputation*

In America Channing's reputation grew steadily in the two decades after his death. By 1872 the collected works had gone through twenty-two editions, and William Henry Channing's *Memoir* (1848) reached ten editions two years later. The centenary of Channing's birth was celebrated in Brooklyn, London, and Liverpool by leading Unitarians, who continued to find in Channing's devotion to liberal principles of Christianity and purity of life examples to be praised and followed. By the century's end there was an almost complete lull in interest, but it was disturbed for a time by John White Chadwick's fine biography in 1903. From then until the past decade, Channing was known chiefly because of his association in one way or another with the names of younger contemporaries who made more dramatic, if not always more distinguished, contributions to American culture.

Now through the publication of several studies of Channing's thought and influence at mid-century, considerable new material has been produced to shed more light on the mystery of Channing's power to exercise widespread influence over his local community, the nation at large, and countries widely separated from America in traditions and culture. The mystery is not entirely dispelled because there are qualities about this shy, reserved man—whom Van Wyck Brooks has called "the impassioned little saint with the burning heart"—that elude the biographer today just as they escaped the contemporary who was forced to admit that "Channing could never be reported." But it is clearer now than it has ever been before that Channing did not accidentally happen upon his ideas of liberty, rational Christianity, and self-reliance. Although the way to religious liberalism had been charted before him by the Arminians, it was Channing's task to join the rational principles of the Enlightenment to the romantic faith in man of the new nation and to build upon the current doctrine of natural rights a firm structure of belief in man's capacity to improve himself indefinitely in a free land.

It should not be forgotten for a moment that Channing was a minister of a group whose popularity was certainly not above question during the first half of the nineteenth century and that his entire career was spent in Boston, a rather conservative city without any great desire to be jarred from traditional patterns into new and bold experiments. Yet Matthew Arnold's powers of man and moment found in Channing alone the moral conviction of serenity of vision to draw both Unitarianism and Boston into the center of early nineteenth-century social, political, and religious activity. Many surpassed him in one way or another: some in intellectual power; some in the power of the spoken word; many in the felicity of prose expression; but no one stood above him in the power to arouse enthusiasm and to compel belief in the exciting doctrine of human improvement.

Notes and References

For the purpose of brevity, the following abbreviations have been used:

AUA — American Unitarian Association, Boston, Massachusetts
Channing Papers — Manuscript Collection of Henry Morse Channing, Sherborn, Massachusetts
MHS — Massachusetts Historical Society, Boston, Massachusetts
Norton Papers — Andrews Norton Papers, Houghton Library, Harvard University, Cambridge, Massachusetts
RIHS — Rhode Island Historical Society, Providence, Rhode Island
RWE — Ralph Waldo Emerson
WEC — William Ellery Channing
WHC — William Henry Channing

Chapter One

1. William H. Channing, *Memoir of William Ellery Channing* (Boston, 1848), I, 6. First child died in infancy. Frances Dana and Anna preceded William. See genealogy in Newport Historical Society Library.
2. Letter to Eloise Payne, April, 1810 (AUA).
3. See Allston's portrait (1800) in Redwood Library, Newport.
4. WHC, *Memoir*, I, 40.
5. George G. Channing, *Early Recollections of Newport, R. I.* (Newport, 1868), p. 34.
6. William Updike, *Memoirs of the Rhode-Island Bar* (Boston, 1842), p. 99.
7. Edward T. Channing, *Life of William Ellery* (Boston, 1837), p. 137.
8. *Ibid.*, p. 135.
9. William E. Channing, *The Works of William E. Channing, D. D.* (Boston, 1848), IV, 341.
10. After Stiles went to Yale, his congregation worshiped with Hopkins in the years 1780-1786.
11. WHC, *Memoir*, I, 33.
12. *Ibid.*, pp. 34-35.

13. F. B. Dexter, *Biographical Sketches of the Graduates of Yale College* (New York, 1907), IV, 183-86.

14. Channing was the second youngest in his class. See Sidney Willard, *Memories of Youth and Manhood* (Cambridge, 1855), II, 8-60, for information about the class of 1798. See also Harvard College Archives, *Records of the College Faculty*, VI (1788-1797), 251.

15. WHC, *Memoir*, I, 45.

16. Harvard College Archives, *Library Charging List*, 1795-1798.

17. WHC, *Memoir*, I, 66.

18. For a clear exposition of the moral liberalism of Professor Tappan, who influenced Channing's entire career at Harvard, read Tappan's *Sermons on Important Subjects* (Cambridge, 1807), *passim*. Hutcheson's *An Inquiry into the Original of Our Ideas and Virtue* (1725) succeeded Henry More's *Enchiridion Ethicum* as the ethics text in use at Harvard. See Benjamin Rand, "Philosophical Instruction in Harvard University from 1636 to 1900," *Harvard Graduates' Magazinue*, XXXVII (Sept., 1928).

19. WHC, *Memoir*, I, 64.

20. H. W. L. Dana, "Allston at Harvard, 1796-1800," *Cambridge Historical Society Publication*, XXIX (1948), 13-33.

21. WHC, *Memoir*, I, 60.

22. These axioms appear in Edward Herbert of Cherbury's *Ancient Religion of the Hebrews*, trans. by William Lewis (London, 1705), pp. 3-4. The list later became a standard part of treatises dealing with deism. See Herbert Morais, *Deism in Eighteenth Century America* (New York, 1934).

23. Richard Watson (1738-1816), bishop of Llandaff, replied to Paine in 1796.

24. See the comments of Daniel White, Channing's classmate, in WHC, *Memoir*, I, 61-62.

25. WHC, *Memoir*, I, 69-70.

26. *Ibid.*, p. 85.

27. *U.S. Magazine and Democratic Review*, IX (October, 1841), 317.

28. WHC, *Memoir*, I, 100.

29. *Ibid.*, p. 106.

30. *Ibid.*, p. 108.

31. *Ibid.*, p. 123.

32. *Ibid.*, p. 134.

33. For reading habits, see WEC, *Works*, I, 167-215. For comments on English theology and the Establishment, read *passim*, *Correspondence of William Ellery Channing, D.D., and Lucy Aikin* (1826-1842), edited by Anna Le Breton (Boston, 1874).

34. WHC, *Memoir*, I, 176.

35. *Ibid.*, p. 206.

36. *The Monthly Anthology*, I (November, 1804), 102.

37. For a contemporary liberal account of the controversy, see *Diary of William Bentley* (4 vols.; Salem: the Essex Institute, 1904-1914), III.

38. *A Sermon Delivered at the Ordination of the Reverend John Codman* (Boston, 1808), pp. 16-17. Channing did not include this sermon in his collected works, perhaps because he did not consider it representative of his theology.

39. WHC, *Memoir*, I, 253.

40. Robert L. Patterson, *The Philosophy of William Ellery Channing* (New York, 1952), p. 159.

41. WHC, *Memoir*, I, 254.

42. *A Sermon Preached in Boston, August 20, 1812* (Boston, 1812), p. 11. Extracts from this sermon are reprinted in WEC, *Works*, V, 411-22.

43. Remarks appeared in an article in the *Christian Examiner* (May, 1829). Article is reprinted in WEC, *Works*, I, 333-67. See Henry Adams, *Documents Relating to New England Federalism* (Boston, 1877) for discussion of the Hartford delegates and their threats of secession.

44. WEC, *Works*, I, 365.

45. *Diary of Wiliam Bentley*, III.

46. E. A. Parks, *Memoir of Nathanael Emmons* (Boston, 1861), p. 163.

47. See MS letter (AUA), January 11, 1813. Also letter from WEC to William Ellery, July 2, 1813.

48. Jedidiah Morse (1761-1826) entered Yale in 1779, where he came under Ezra Stiles' influence. Later he became a New Light Calvinist. In 1784 his *Geography Made Easy* was the first book of its kind to be published in America. In the 1790's he was active in running down French infidelity because he hoped to unite Hopkinsians, moderates, and liberals against a common enemy. After the turn of the century, however, he was an implacable foe of those whose religion failed to meet his standards. See James K. Morse, *Jedidiah Morse, A Champion of New England Orthodoxy* (New York, 1939).

49. *A Letter to the Reverend Samuel C. Thacher* (Boston, 1815), pp. 13-14. See reprint in WHC, *Memoir*, I, 381-96.

50. *A Letter*, p. 23.

51. For a contemporary view of the Worcester-Channing contest, see *A Candid and Contemporary Review of the Late Correspond-*

ence of the Reverend Dr. Worcester with the Reverend William E. Channing (Boston, 1817).

52. Reprinted in WEC, *Works*, V, 373-91.

53. John Lowell, *Are You a Christian or a Calvinist?* (Boston, 1815), pp. 15-16.

54. "Unitarian Christianity," *Works*, III, 59-103.

55. For a full account of the Unitarian Controversy and an excellent bibliography, see E. H. Gillette, "History and Literature of the Unitarian Controversy," *The Historical Magazine*, IX (April, 1871), 221-324.

56. For details of the Dedham decision, see Jacob C. Meyer, *Church and State in Massachusetts from 1740 to 1833* (Cleveland, 1930), pp. 174-80.

57. WHC, *Memoir*, II, 191.

58. Quoted from Wordsworth, *ibid.*, p. 218.

59. *Ibid.*, p. 221.

60. Quoted from WEC in Elizabeth Peabody's *Reminiscences of Reverend William Ellery Channing, D.D.* (Boston, 1880), p. 96.

61. Samuel Taylor Coleridge, *Letters*, ed. E. H. Coleridge (Boston, 1895), p. 676.

62. S. T. Coleridge, *Aids to Reflection* (London, 1913), p. 103.

63. For elaboration of Coleridge's view, see his *On the Constitution of Church and State* (1830). See also C. R. Sanders, *Coleridge and the Broad Church Movement* (Durham, 1942).

64. WHC, *Memoir*, II, 240.

65. *Ibid.*, p. 343.

66. Ralph Rusk, *The Life of Ralph Waldo Emerson* (New York, 1949), p. 103.

67. MS letter from Mrs. S. J. Hale to Edward Everett, March 28, 1826 (MHS).

68. "Address on the Anniversary of Emancipation in the British West-Indies," *Works*, VI, 381.

69. MS letter from WEC to Andrews Norton, January 24, 1831 (Norton Papers).

70. MS letter from WEC to Andrews Norton, April 1, 1831 (Norton Papers).

71. Peabody, *Reminiscences*, p. 358.

72. Maria Chapman (ed.), *Harriet Martineau's Autobiography* (Boston, 1877), II, 272-73.

73. Harriet Martineau, *Retrospect of Western Travel*, II, 79.

74. Samuel May, *Some Recollections of Our Antislavery Conflict* (Boston, 1869), p. 172.

75. *Ibid.*, pp. 173, 175.

76. *Ibid.*, p. 175.
77. Charles F. Adams (ed.), *Memoirs of John Quincy Adams* (Philadelphia, 1876), IX, 266.
78. MS letter from WEC to Elizabeth Peabody, March 23, 1828 (AUA library).
79. WHC, *Memoir*, III, 215.
80. *Ibid.*, p. 229.
81. WEC, *Works,* VI, 177.
82. *Ibid.*, p. 417.
83. *Ibid.*, p. 419.
84. *Ibid.*
85. Theodore Parker, *An Humble Tribute to the Memory of William Ellery Channing, D.D.* (Boston, 1842), pp. 9, 25.

Chapter Two

1. For biographical data, see William B. Sprague, *Annals of the American Pulpit* (New York, 1857-1869); Clifford K. Shipton, *Sibley's Harvard Graduates* (Cambridge and Boston, 1933-1951), Vols. IV-VIII.
2. Perry Miller, "Individualism and the New England Tradition," *The Journal of Liberal Religion,* IV (Summer, 1942), 9.
3. Perry Miller, *Jonathan Edwards* (New York, 1959), pp. 108-9.
4. For a sound treatment of the Great Awakening, especially its social and political aspects, see Conrad Wright, *The Beginnings of Unitarianism in America* (Boston, 1955), pp. 28-59. This source is excellent for the history of Arminianism up to the time of Channing. See also E. S. Gaustad, *The Great Awakening in New England* (New York, 1957).
5. Comparison of the two approaches can be made from Chauncy's *Seasonable Thoughts on the State of Religion* (1743) and Edwards' *A Treatise Concerning the Religious Affections* (1746). See also Miller, *Jonathan Edwards*, pp. 165-95.
6. The list of books read by Channing as an undergraduate and the reading lists he sometimes recommended to beginning students in divinity do not differ much from those used by the Arminians in 1750.
7. John Bass, *A True Narrative of an Unhappy Contention in the Church at Ashford* (Boston, 1751), pp. 26, 27.
8. See Jonathan Mayhew, *Seven Sermons Delivered at the Boston Lecture* (Boston, 1749).
9. *Ibid.*, p. 31.

10. Charles Chauncy, *Five Dissertations on the Scripture Account of the Fall and Its Consequences* (London, 1785), p. 33.

11. Gad Hitchcock, *Natural Religion Aided by Revelation and Perfected in Christianity* (Boston, 1779), p. 15.

12. See above, p. 23, note 18.

13. Though prepared in the 1760's, the treatise was not published until 1784. See Wright, *op. cit.*, pp. 187-93, for a detailed explanation of reasons for delay.

14. James Freeman, *Sermons on Particular Occasions* (Boston, 1821), pp. 235, 236.

15. Samuel Hopkins, *The Importance and Necessity of Christians considering Jesus Christ in the Extent of His High Glorious Character* (Boston, 1768), p. 27. Sermon is reprinted in WEC, *Works* (Boston, 1854), III, 501-17.

16. See Wright, *op. cit.*, pp. 200-17 for details.

17. *The Works of John Adams* (Boston, 1850), I, 30, 32.

18. See Harry Hayden Clark, *Thomas Paine* (New York, 1944) for an excellent introduction to deism and especially Paine's role.

19. See text, p. 24.

20. See G. H. Koch, *Republican Religion* (New York, 1933) and Herbert H. Morais, *Deism in Eighteenth Century America* (New York, 1934) for extensive treatments of deistic activity.

21. Vernon Stauffer, *New England and the Bavarian Illuminati* (New York, 1918), pp. 229-360.

22. WHC, *Memoir*, I, 73.

23. *Ibid.*, p. 78.

24. James Walker, *Memoir of Hon. Daniel Appleton White* (Boston, 1863), pp. 8-9.

25. Francis Hutcheson, *An Inquiry into the Original of our Ideas of Beauty and Virtue* (2nd ed.; London, 1726), p. 134.

26. WHC, *Memoir*, I, 66. See also Anna L. Le Breton, *Correspondence of William Ellery Channing, D.D. and Lucy Aikin, From 1826 to 1842* (Boston, 1874), p. 82, for corroboration.

27. Richard Price, *A Review of the Principal Questions and Difficulties in Morals* (2nd ed.; London, 1769), pp. 56-57.

28. *Ibid.*, p. 59.

29. *Ibid.*, p. 92.

30. Price claims that virtue is "an unalterable and indispensable law" and "the source and guide of all the actions of the Deity himself," *ibid.*, p. 178.

31. See WEC, *Works*, III, 64-69; IV, 34-37.

32. Compare, for example, Price's "A rational agent, void of all moral judgment, incapable of perceiving a difference, in respect of fitness and unfitness to be performed between any actions . . .

is not possible to be conceived of" (*op. cit.*, p. 71), and Channing's "A being so constituted as to see baseness in disinterested love and venerableness in malignity would be an inconceivable monster" (*The Works of William E. Channing, D.D.* [Boston, 1901], p. 943).

33. Price, *op. cit.*, p. 377.

34. John Weiss, *Life and Correspondence of Theodore Parker* (New York, 1864), I, 108.

35. Price, *op. cit.*, p. 423.

36. Adam Ferguson, *An Essay on the History of Civil Society* (London, 1782), p. 89.

37. See text, pp. 28, 29.

38. WHC, *Memoir*, I, 137-38; WEC, *Works*, IV, 347-54.

39. *Works*, IV, 342-43.

40. *Ibid.*, p. 343.

41. Hopkins believed in the use of means, but unless man repented and submitted to God's grace, such use only added to his guilt. See *Sketches of the Life of the Late Rev. Samuel Hopkins, D.D.* (Hartford, 1805), pp. 45-46.

42. Manuscript of this course of study is in possession of the Harvard Divinity School.

43. Sydney Ahlstrom, "The Scottish Philosophy and American Theology," *Church History*, XXIV, 257-69. Contains an excellent account of summary views that are related in text to Channing.

44. *Ibid.*

45. WEC, *Works* (Boston, 1901), p. 981.

46. Manuscript in possession of Meadville Seminary Library, Chicago. Quoted in Patterson, *op. cit.*, p. 228.

47. Dudleian lecture at Harvard (1821) on "The Evidences of Revealed Religion" in WEC, *Works*, III, 105-36.

48. WEC, *Works*, I, 76-77; IV, 142-46.

49. *Ibid.*, III, 275.

50. *Ibid.*, IV, 35, 36.

51. *Ibid.*, p. 109.

52. WEC to Eloise Payne, December 29, 1812. Manuscript letter in AUA.

53. See Patterson, *op. cit.*, pp. 29-60, for detailed analysis of Lockean views and relationship to Channing.

54. WEC, *Works*, III, 95.

55. *Ibid.*, IV, 32.

56. *Ibid.*, p. 110.

57. *Ibid.*, p. 41.

58. Manuscript letter, January 11, 1813, in AUA. Reprinted in WHC, *Memoir*, I, 355-57.

59. WHC, *ibid.*, p. 384.
60. *Ibid.*, p. 161.
61. WEC, *Works*, III, 75-77.
62. *Ibid.*, IV, 188. See Patterson, *op. cit.*, pp. 84-86, 159-67, 193-94, for defense of "essential sameness," Channing's unique contribution to Christian theology.
63. WEC, *Works*, III, 82-83.
64. *Ibid.*, I, 229.
65. Emerson and Forbes, *The Journals of Ralph Waldo Emerson* (Boston and New York, 1909-1914), I, 361.
66. WHC, *Memoir*, II, 248.
67. WEC, *Works*, III, 146.
68. *Ibid.*, p. 197.
69. Le Breton, *Correspondence*, p. 9.
70. WEC, *Works*, III, 207, 209, 210.
71. *Ibid.*, p. 209.
72. *Ibid.*, pp. 233, 234, 235.
73. *Spirit of the Pilgrims*, I (Sept. 10, 1828), pp. 667-68.
74. "Nature is rich and inexhaustible, and pours out her fine forms with every diversity of hue and outline—and the soul is even more rich and various than outward nature, has more of individuality." Manuscript letter to Mrs. Catherine Sedgwick, Aug. 23, 1827 (Channing Papers).
75. WEC, *Works*, I, 50.
76. *Ibid.*, III, 233.
77. *Ibid.*, IV, 83.
78. *Ibid.*, III, 310.
79. *Ibid.*, II, 359.
80. *Ibid.*, V, 304.
81. *Ibid.*, VI, 204-5.

Chapter Three

1. Le Breton, *Correspondence*, p. 224. (Letter containing remarks is dated August, 1834.)
2. See text, pp. 17-18, 24-25.
3. WHC, *Memoir*, I, 86.
4. *Ibid.*, pp. 156-57.
5. *Ibid.*, p. 86.
6. See R. G. Collingwood, *The Idea of History* (Oxford, 1946), pp. 83-86, for discussion of this subject.
7. WHC, *Memoir*, II, 404.
8. *Ibid.*, I, 319.
9. WEC, *Works*, IV, 238.

10. *Ibid.,* I, 363.

11. *Ibid.,* V, 412.

12. WHC, *Memoir,* II, 80.

13. *Ibid.,* p. 81.

14. WEC, *Works,* I, 159.

15. WHC, *Memoir,* II, 226, 227.

16. *Ibid.,* p. 227.

17. *Ibid.,* p. 249.

18. Arthur M. Schlesinger, Jr., *The Age of Jackson* (New York, 1945), p. 146.

19. WHC, *Memoir,* III, 26.

20. WEC, *Works,* I, 144.

21. *Ibid.,* p. 163.

22. *Ibid.,* p. 344.

23. According to Channing's brother-in-law, Washington Allston, "Whatever, then, impresses the mind *as* truth, *is* truth until it can be shown to be false." R. H. Dana, Jr. (ed.), *Lectures on Art and Poems* (Cambridge, 1850), p. 253.

24. Ferguson, *op. cit.,* p. 95.

25. *Ibid.,* p. 101.

26. Le Breton, *Correspondence,* p. 204.

27. MS letter from WEC to Nathan Appleton, Feb. 25, 1833 (MHS).

28. See Le Breton, *Correspondence,* pp. 122, 131, 142, 156, 234, 273, *passim.*

29. *Ibid.,* p. 111.

30. *Ibid.,* p. 63.

31. *Ibid.,* p. 125; WEC, *Works,* I, 362.

32. WHC, *Memoir,* III, 261.

33. *Ibid.,* p. 124.

34. WEC, *Works,* VI, 82; V, 113; WHC, *Memoir,* III, 261.

35. WHC, *Memoir,* III, 263.

36. Entry, June 18, 1834, *The Journals of Ralph Waldo Emerson,* ed. by Edward Waldo Emerson and Waldo Emerson Forbes (Boston, 1909-14).

37. WHC, *Memoir,* III, 263.

38. Compare remarks on party spirit in 1812 (WHC, *Memoir,* I, 325) with those on political parties and party leadership in 1836-1842 (WHC, *Memoir,* III, 260-63).

39. WHC, *Memoir,* III, 260.

40. Le Breton, *Correspondence,* p. 63.

41. WHC, *Memoir,* III, 300-3.

42. Le Breton, *Correspondence,* p. 62.

43. *Ibid.,* p. 223.

44. WEC, *Works*, VI, 348; WHC, *Memoir*, III, 252.

45. Le Breton, *Correspondence*, p. 144; WHC, *Memoir*, III, 254.

46. Although Channing's emphasis is perhaps unusual, he was in the main stream of Enlightenment thought as far as education for civic responsibility was concerned. From 1820 on, the American public school was expected to train not only for civic duty but for everything under the sun.

47. WHC, *Memoir*, III, 275.

48. WEC, *Works*, IV, 83.

49. *Ibid.*, p. 76.

50. *Ibid.*, p. 78.

51. *Ibid.*, II, 26. For fuller exposition of this argument and of Channing's conception of natural rights, see Patterson, *op. cit.*, pp. 97-137.

52. WEC, *Works*, IV, 91.

53. *Ibid.*, II, 36.

54. *Ibid.*, p. 34.

55. *Ibid.*, p. 35.

56. *Ibid.*, VI, 343.

Chapter Four

1. See journal entries concerning better housing, evils of prostitution, temperance, education in WHC, *Memoir*, I, 232-34. See also sermon on *Religion a Social Principle* (Boston, 1820).

2. WEC, *Works* (Boston, 1901), p. 943.

3. WEC, *Works*, III, 14.

4. *Religion a Social Principle*, p. 7; *Works*, II, 13.

5. *Ibid.*, V, 166.

6. "William Ellery Channing," *The U.S. Magazine and Democratic Review*, XII (May, 1843), 525.

7. *Ibid.*, pp. 166-67.

8. WEC, *Works*, I, 374.

9. MS letter to Eloise Payne dated June 20, 1809 (Channing Papers). Also MS letter dated Aug. 21, 1811 (AUA).

10. WHC, *Memoir*, II, 15-17.

11. *Ibid.*, II, 69-70.

12. *Ibid.*, p. 312.

13. *Ibid.*, pp. 318, 328-34.

14. *Ibid.*, p. 303.

15. *Ibid.*, V, 118.

16. *Ibid.*, p. 119.

17. *Ibid.*, III, 45.

18. *Ibid.*, V, 136.

19. Le Breton, *Correspondence*, p. 348.
20. *Ibid.*
21. WHC, *Memoir*, II, 111-16.
22. See Louis H. Warner, "Channing and Cheverus: A Study in Early New England Tolerance," *Christian Register* (May 4, 1939), 296-99.
23. See John Commons, *et al.*, *History of Labor in the United States* (New York, 1918), I, 158.
24. See Josiah Quincy, *A Municipal History of the Town and City of Boston* (Boston, 1852), p. 34 f. Edward Everett Hale's *A New England Boyhood* (New York, 1893) presents a graphic picture of Boston in the late 1820's and 1830's.
25. WEC, *Works*, III, 157-58.
26. WHC, *Memoir*, III, 74-77.
27. WEC, *Works*, V, 192.
28. Le Breton, *Correspondence*, p. 61.
29. Letter dated July 12, 1831, WHC, *Memoir*, III, 111.
30. WEC, *Works*, II, 315.
31. WHC, *Memoir*, III, 110.
32. For details concerning Tuckerman's work, see WEC, *Works*, VI, 91-146, and Daniel T. McColgan, *Joseph Tuckerman, Pioneer in American Social Work* (Washington, 1940).
33. WHC, *Memoir*, III, 51.
34. *Ibid.*, p. 53.
35. *Ibid.*, p. 68.
36. *Ibid.*, p. 69.
37. WEC, *Works*, IV, 267.
38. See Aikin Correspondence and manuscript letters in RIHS, MHS, and WHC, *Memoir*, III, 134-241.
39. See text, p. 45.
40. See letter dated Oct. 20, 1834, in WHC, *Memoir*, III, 165; William Lloyd Garrison, *The Liberator*, VI (Feb. 27, 1836), 35.
41. Letter in WHC, *Memoir*, III, 154-55.
42. *The U.S. Magazine and Democratic Review*, XII (May, 1834), 526.
43. WEC, *Works*, II, 15-16.
44. *Ibid.*, pp. 26, 27. For opposing theory of "natural" slavery, see W. Ashley, *The Theory of Natural Slavery According to Aristotle and St. Thomas*, pp. 28-33.
45. WEC, *Works*, II, 98.
46. *Ibid.*, p. 116.
47. *Ibid.*
48. Garrison, *The Liberator*, VI (Feb. 27, 1836), 35. Letter from Miss Grimké to WEC, June, 1837 (Channing Papers).

49. *Remarks on Dr. Channing's Slavery by A Citizen of Massachusetts* (Boston, 1835), p. 14.

50. May, *op. cit.*, p. 176.

51. Manuscript letter in AUA library. Also reprinted in S. T. Pickard's *The Life and Letters of John Greenleaf Whittier* (Boston, 1894).

Chapter Five

1. Orville Dewey, *Discourse on the Character and Writings of Rev. William E. Channing, D.D.* (New York, 1843), pp. 7, 29.

2. WHC, *Memoir*, II, 330. Letter dated May 5, 1834.

3. WEC, *Works*, II, 334.

4. *Ibid.*, p. 372.

5. Le Breton, *Correspondence*, p. 54.

6. WEC, *Works*, I, 37.

7. *Ibid.*, VI, 156; Peabody, *Reminiscences*, p. 75.

8. Le Breton, *Correspondence*, p. 235.

9. Peabody, *Reminiscences*, p. 339.

10. Le Breton, *Correspondence*, p. 85.

11. Peabody, *Reminiscences*, p. 267.

12. Le Breton, *Correspondence*, p. 234.

13. *Ibid.*, p. 158.

14. *Ibid.*, p. 234; WHC, *Memoir*, II, 351.

15. Peabody, *Reminiscences*, pp. 336-37.

16. WHC, *Memoir*, II, 403.

17. Manuscript and typewritten transcription are possession of Meadville Seminary Library, Chicago.

18. WHC, *Memoir*, I, 262, 263.

19. *Ibid.*, p. 264.

20. Dugald Stewart (1753-1828) and Archibald Alison (1757-1839) were largely responsible for the change in aesthetic theory within the Common Sense group that paved the way for writers like Coleridge. Alison replaced the concept of the intrinsic beauty of objects with the Platonic concept of subjectivity. See also Sidney Ahlstrom, "The Scottish Philosophy and American Theology," *Church History*, XXIV (1955), 257-72.

21. Ernest Renan, *Leaders of Christian and Anti-Christian Thought* (London, 1891), p. 13. See Channing's own remark about "accidental" authorship in letter to Joanna Baillie, May 5, 1834. WHC, *Memoir*, II, 330.

22. See Alexander H. Everett, "Tone of British Criticism," *North American Review*, XXXI (July, 1830), 26-66. According

Notes and References

to Everett: "The *Quarterly* reviles us, the *Edinburgh* sneers at us, *Blackwood* bullies us."

23. For Emerson's views, see "Historic Notes," *op. cit.*, p. 321; *Journals*, IV, 38; VI, 105, 284-85; *Letters*, I, 291, 344 ff.

24. RWE, *Works*, X, 320.

25. A complete documentation of English periodical criticism can be found in Robert Spiller's "A Case for W. E. Channing," *New England Quarterly*, XXX (January, 1930), 55-81.

26. *Monthly Magazine*, n.s., VIII (April, 1828), 471-78.

27. *Westminster Review*, X (April, 1828), 98-101.

28. *Edinburgh Review*, L (October, 1829), 132, 133, 139.

29. WEC, *Works*, I, 6, 7.

30. *Ibid.*, p. 68.

31. *Ibid.*, p. 118.

32. *Ibid.*, p. 120.

33. Hazlitt, *op. cit.*, p. 143.

34. RWE, *Works*, X, 320.

35. WEC, *Works*, I, 167.

36. *Ibid.*, p. 168.

37. *Ibid.*, p. 212.

38. *Westminster Review*, XII (April, 1830), 478.

39. "The Lounger, No. 11," *New Monthly Magazine*, XVIII (May, 1830), 469.

40. *Athenaeum*, II (October 14, 1829), 637-39; III (May 8, 1830), 280-81.

41. *Ibid.*, VIII (June 3, 1835), 9.

42. *North American Review*, XLI (October, 1835), 366.

43. *Fraser's Magazine*, XVII (May, 1838), 627; XVIII (Sept., 1838), 291.

44. WEC, *Works*, I, 21.

45. *Edinburgh Review*, LXIX (April, 1839), 218.

46. *Ibid.*, p. 225.

47. *Ibid.*, p. 229.

48. *Ibid.*

49. Le Breton, *Correspondence*, p. 352.

50. MS letter dated May 8, 1839 (MHS). Author was Harvard-trained, a student of German culture, and former head of famous Round Hill School. At time of writing, author was owner and editor of *New York Review*.

51. WEC, *Works*, I, 244.

52. *Ibid.*, p. 248.

53. *Ibid.*, p. 253.

54. *Ibid.*, p. 270.

55. *Ibid.*, p. 248.

56. *Ibid.*, p. 272.

57. *Ibid.*, p. 247.

58. William Charvat, *The Origins of American Critical Thought*: *1810-1835* (Philadelphia, 1936), pp. 198-201.

59. WEC, *Works*, II, 366.

60. *Ibid.*, VI, 155-56.

61. *Ibid.*, I, v.

62. RWE, *Journals*, VI, 106.

Chapter Six

1. The influence of most of these women can be generally traced in William Henry Channing's *Memoir*. The Aikin letters need no further comment, but Channing's correspondence with Catherine Sedgwick, which extends from the late 1820's to the year of his death, shows a decided change in Miss Sedgwick's romantic novels as a result of Channing's "moral" advice. The Sedgwick correspondence is in the possession of Henry M. Channing, Sherborn, Mass.

2. For details of these associations, see *Memoir of Samuel May* (Boston, 1873); *Autobiography and Letters of Orville Dewey, D.D.* (Boston, 1883); and *Ezra Stiles Gannett, A Memoir* (Boston, 1875).

3. Ralph Rusk (ed.), *The Letters of Ralph Waldo Emerson* (New York, 1939), I, 138. Also RWE, *Journals*, I, 291.

4. James E. Cabot, *A Memoir of Ralph Waldo Emerson* (Boston and New York, 1887), I, 102.

5. RWE, *Journals*, II, 29.

6. Eliza Lee Follen, *The Works of Charles Follen with a Memoir of His Life* (Boston, 1841), I, 162 f.

7. See Orie Long, *Literary Pioneers* (Cambridge, 1935), pp. 3-62, for a detailed account of Ticknor's efforts to rebuild the Harvard curriculum to take advantage of European insights. *Life, Letters, and Journals*, ed. by Anna Ticknor and George Hillard (2 vols.; Boston, 1880) contains Channing-Ticknor correspondence.

8. RWE, "Historic Notes of Life and Letters in New England," *Works*, III, 321.

9. Odell Shepard, *The Journals of Bronson Alcott* (Boston, 1838), p. 15. Hereafter referred to as Alcott, *Journals*.

10. *Ibid.*, p. 19.

11. Helen E. Marshall, *Dorothea Dix, Forgotten Samaritan* (Chapel Hill, 1937), pp. 86-87. Details of Channing's role in encouraging Miss Dix to undertake her work among criminals and mentally ill.

12. Alcott, *Journals*, p. 32.
13. *New England Magazine*, IV (March, 1833), 241.
14. *Ibid.* (May, 1833), 409-10.
15. George Ripley, "Philosophic Thought in Boston," *The Memorial History of Boston*, ed. by Justin Winsor (Boston, 1881), IV, 300.
16. *Works of Orestes Brownson*, ed. H. F. Brownson (Detroit, 1882-1902), IV, 46.
17. *The Philanthropist*, II, 86.
18. Letter, dated Jan. 11, 1834, in H. F. Brownson, *Orestes A. Brownson's Early Life* (Detroit, 1898), pp. 106-8.
19. *Ibid.*, p. 105.
20. For Brownson's connection with the working-class movement, see Arthur M. Schlesinger, Jr., *Orestes A. Brownson: A Pilgrim's Progress* (Boston, 1934), pp. 20-23.
21. Alcott, *Journals*, pp. 77-78.
22. *Ibid.*, pp. 84-86.
23. So regarded in the circles in which Andrews Norton was the hierophant. See letter from John Brazer to Andrews Norton, Nov. 7, 1836 (Norton Papers).
24. Charles E. Norton (ed.), *The Correspondence of Thomas Carlyle and Ralph Waldo Emerson* (Boston, 1883), I, 47 f.
25. *Ibid.*, p. 65 f.
26. WEC, *Works*, III, 243.
27. Peabody, *Reminiscences*, p. 381.
28. The date was September 19, 1836. See RWE, *Journals*, IV, 85-87.
29. For details, see O. B. Frothingham, *Theodore Parker: A Biography* (Boston, 1874), pp. 96-99.
30. WHC, *Memoir*, III, 55.
31. Miss Peabody's translation of Gérando's work was published in Boston in 1832. Channing corresponded frequently with Gérando during the 1830's, securing from him and Jean Charles Sismondi, his countryman, most of his information about reform movements on the continent.
32. Clarke, Henry Channing, and Christopher Cranch used the *Western Messenger* to bring to the West the latest developments in thought and social action in the East. When criticism was directed against Emerson for his Divinity School Address, they were quick to defend him. The "New School of Emerson," they claimed, was really led by Dr. Channing "because from him has come the strongest impulse to independent thought, to earnest self-supported activity." Perry Miller, *The Transcendentalists* (Cambridge, 1950), p. 204.

33. See Henry's Manifesto, entitled "An Ideal of Humanity," in *The Western Messenger,* VIII (May, 1840), 1-8.

34. Letter is dated Aug. 19, 1837, WHC, *Memoir,* III, 89.

35. For Mann's struggles to organize the school system, see Raymond B. Culver, *Horace Mann and Religion in the Massachusetts Public Schools* (New Haven, 1929).

36. For a description of the meeting see the entry in Parker's Journal for Feb. 8, 1838, in Frothingham, *Theodore Parker,* p. 97.

37. WEC, *Works,* III, 274.

38. Peabody, *Reminiscences,* pp. 379-80.

39. *Ibid.,* p. 379.

40. Letter dated July 28, 1841, *ibid.,* p. 429.

41. Miller, *The Transcendentalists,* p. 490.

42. Letter dated July 6, 1841, Peabody, *op. cit.,* p. 423.

43. Letter dated July 28, 1841, *ibid.,* p. 429.

44. *Ibid.,* p. 403.

45. Rusk, *The Letters of Ralph Waldo Emerson,* II, 294.

46. Letter dated Sept., 1840, Peabody, *op. cit.,* p. 414.

47. Norton's address had been delivered at the Divinity School in 1839 as an answer to Emerson. Ripley decried Norton's contentions in a series of letters in the Boston press that same year.

48. Letter to James Martineau, Sept. 10, 1841, WHC, *Memoir,* II, 399.

49. See "Remarks on Associations" in WEC, *Works,* I, 281-332.

50. See Octavius Frothingham, *George Ripley* (Boston, 1882), p. 303.

51. Letter dated Feb. 27, 1841, WHC, *Memoir,* III, 119.

52. Essay appeared in *Boston Quarterly Review,* III (July, 1840). A. M. Schlesinger, Jr., calls it "perhaps the best study of society written by an American before the Civil War." *Orestes Brownson* (Boston, 1939), p. 96. Whigs made political capital out of it since Brownson was a Democrat and the essay came out just before the presidential election.

53. WHC, *Memoir,* II, 123-24.

54. *Ibid.,* p. 124.

55. Letter dated June 10, 1842, in H. F. Brownson, *Early Life,* p. 443. *Mediatorial Life* printed in Boston, 1842. Reprinted in *Brownson's Works,* IV.

56. H. F. Brownson, *Early Life,* pp. 443-44.

57. Journal entry for April 16, 1841, in E. H. Hale (ed.), *James Freeman Clarke: Autobiography, Diary and Correspondence* (Boston, 1891), p. 161.

58. For a good account of the Chardon Street Convention, see Emerson's article in the *Dial,* III (1840), 100.

59. Peabody, *Reminiscences,* p. 371.
60. MS letter to Channing dated Oct. 12, 1834 (RIHS).
61. Peabody, *Reminiscences,* p. 365.
62. *Ibid.*
63. Unlike most of the Unitarians, Channing did not identify transcendentalism with pantheism, although he was certain that Alcott preached pantheistic views. See letter to Elizabeth Peabody dated August, 1841, *Reminiscences,* pp. 431-32.
64. RWE, *Journals,* IV, 87, 108, 239.

Chapter Seven

1. MS letter from Lord Holland dated July 16, 1839 (RIHS).
2. *American Notes for General Circulation* (New York, 1842), p. 13.
3. Siegfried B. Puksat, "Auerbach and Channing," *PMLA,* LXXII (December, 1957), 973.

Selected Bibliography

BIBLIOGRAPHY

No bibliography of Dr. Channing has been published. The entries in volume three of the *Literary History of the United States* (1957) are not exhaustive. The Bibliographic Supplement to the *Literary History* (1959) not only fails to remedy the lack but compounds the error of confusing Dr. Channing with his nephew. In addition, the Supplement refers to "the first full bibliography of Channing's work" in Joseph Blanck's *Bibliography of American Literature* (New Haven, 1957), II, 129-33, a work that omits Dr. Channing and lists the bibliography of William Ellery Channing the poet instead.

TEXT

Correspondence of William Ellery Channing and Lucy Aikin, from 1826 to 1842, ed. by ANNA LETITIA LE BRETON. Boston, 1874.
A Discourse, Delivered in Boston at the Solemn Festival in Commemoration of the Goodness of God in Delivering the Christian World from Military Despotism, June 16, 1814. Cambridge, 1814.
Discourses, Reviews, and Miscellanies. Boston, 1830.
Dr. Channing's Note-Book, Passages from the Unpublished Manuscripts of William Ellery Channing, Selected by His Granddaughter, Grace Ellery Channing. Boston and New York, 1887.
A Letter to the Rev. Samuel C. Thacher, on the Aspersions contained in a Late Number of the Panoplist, on the Ministers of Boston and the Vicinity. Boston, 1815.
[CHANNING, WILLIAM HENRY] *Memoir of William Ellery Channing, with Extracts from His Correspondence and Manuscripts*. 3 vols. Boston, 1848.
Religion, a Social Principle (A Sermon delivered in Federal Street, Boston, December 10, 1820). Boston, 1820.
Remarks on the Rev. Dr. Worcester's Letter to Mr. Channing, on the 'Review of American Unitarianism' in a Late Panoplist. Boston, 1815.

Selected Bibliography

Remarks on the Rev. Dr. Worcester's Second Letter to Mr. Channing, on American Unitarianism. Boston, 1815.

A Sermon Delivered at the Ordination of the Rev. John Codman, to the Pastoral Care of the Second Church of Christ in Dorchester, Dec. 7, 1808. Boston, 1808.

A Sermon, Preached in Boston, April 5, 1810, the Day of the Public Fast. Boston, 1810.

The Works of William E. Channing, D.D. 8th complete edition, with an Introduction. 6 vols. Boston, 1848. (The works were first published in five volumes in 1842; a sixth volume was added in 1843. The collected works went through twenty-two editions, English and American, by 1872.)

The Works of William E. Channing, D.D. With an Introduction. New and Complete Edition, Rearranged. To Which Is Added the Perfect Life. Boston, 1888.

BIOGRAPHY AND CRITICISM

BROOKS, CHARLES T. *William Ellery Channing.* Boston, 1880. Intended as a brief, popular life. Adds several personal reminiscences to *Memoir*. Not interpretative.

[BROUGHAM, HENRY]. Review of Channing's "Milton" in the *Edinburgh Review or Critical Journal,* LXIX (April, 1839), 214-30.

BROWN, ARTHUR W. *Always Young for Liberty.* Syracuse, 1956. Full-length biography emphasizing personal as well as public aspects of Channing's life.

CHADWICK, JOHN WHITE. *William Ellery Channing: Minister of Religion.* Boston and New York, 1903. An excellent biography written by a "liberal" Unitarian.

The Channing Centenary in America, Great Britain, and Ireland, ed. by RUSSEL NEVINS BELLOWS. Boston, 1881. Roundup of choicest eulogistic morsels.

"Channing's Literary and Political Ideas," *Fraser's Magazine,* XVII (May, 1838), 627-35 and XVIII (September, 1838), 286-97. Review of Channing's articles on Milton and Napoleon. Lauds Channing the writer but cannot agree with his religion or politics.

DOWNS, LENTHIEL. "Emerson and Dr. Channing: Two Men from Boston," *New England Quarterly,* XX (December, 1947), 516-34. Assembles tangential contacts of the two men.

EDGELL, DAVID P. *William Ellery Channing: An Intellectual Portrait.* Boston, 1955. A thorough effort to analyze Channing's thought. Sees Channing's role as "synthesizer of intellectual and ethical theories"; plays down 19th-century emphasis on "personality."

HICKS, GRANVILLE. "Dr. Channing and the Creole Case," *The American Historical Review*, XXXVII (April, 1932), 516-25. Article is based on manuscript letters in Rhode Island Historical Society library. Reveals that Channing was a painstaking researcher when he was dealing with matters outside the theological field.

————. "When Dickens Met Channing," *Christian Register*, CVIII (July 18, 1929), 603-4. Based on letter, dated Jan. 29, 1842, from Dickens to Channing. Conclusions are purely circumstantial.

HOLT, ANNE. *William Ellery Channing: His Religious and Social Thought.* London, 1942. Emphasizes Channing's inability to see evil in the world. The author, an Englishwoman, says antislavery struggle shows Channing's view of human nature at its weakest.

LADU, ARTHUR, I. "Channing and Transcendentalism," *American Literature*, XI (May, 1939), 129-37. Author concludes that Channing was no transcendentalist.

MOOD, FULMER and HICKS, GRANVILLE. "Letters to Dr. Channing on Slavery and the Annexation of Texas, 1837," *New England Quarterly*, V (1932), 587-601. Based on letters in Rhode Island Historical Library. Presents evidence of Channing's "worldly" connections. Reveals that he was not a "cloistered" idealist.

PARKER, THEODORE. *An Humble Tribute to the Memory of William Ellery Channing, D.D.* Boston, 1842. An excellent account of Channing's liberalism by a man who knew him well during the last five years of Channing's life.

PATTERSON, ROBERT L. *The Philosophy of William Ellery Channing.* New York, 1952. Thorough treatment of Channing's idea of "essential sameness." Indispensable for technical knowledge of Channing's theological ideas.

PEABODY, ELIZABETH P. *Reminiscences of William Ellery Channing, D.D.* Boston, 1880. Contains valuable primary material about Channing from 1825 to 1842. Details of time and place often inaccurate. Invaluable source of Channing's letters.

REINHARDT, JOHN E. "The Evolution of William Ellery Channing's Sociopolitical Ideas," *American Literature*, XXVI (1954), 155-65. Although Channing's sociopolitical ideas grew more liberal, his final views of American society and government "led to personal disillusionment."

Selected Bibliography

SCHNEIDER, HERBERT W. "The Intellectual Background of William
Ellery Channing," *Church History,* VII (March, 1938), 3-24.
Takes point of view that Channing is the culmination of the
American Enlightenment. Says he "gave to purely practical
reform an adequate theoretical basis."
SPILLER, ROBERT E. "A Case for William Ellery Channing," *New
England Quarterly,* III (January, 1930), 55-81. Presents
evidence to show that Channing was ranked with Irving
and Cooper as one of the finest American writers.
WHITEHEAD, CHARLES. "The Literary Career of William Ellery
Channing," *Bentley's Miscellany,* XXV (1849), 88-90. A neat
summary of Channing's reputation in England during the
years 1825 to 1849.

BACKGROUND

AIKIN, LUCY. *Memoirs, Miscellanies and Letters of the Late Lucy
Aikin,* ed. by PHILIP H. LE BRETON. London, 1864. Gives a
brief account of Miss Aikin's career and reprints letters to
Channing, written during years 1826-1842.
BALDWIN, ALICE. *The New England Clergy and the American
Revolution.* Durham, 1928. Shows that clergy were not a class
apart but took an active share in discussing all the "rights"
asserted in the Declaration of Independence.
BARNES, GILBERT H. *The Antislavery Impulse, 1830-1844.* New
York, 1933. An excellent treatment of the religious basis of
the antislavery movement.
BENTLEY, WILLIAM. *The Diary of William Bentley* (1759-1819).
4 vols. Salem, 1905-1914. Detailed account of all aspects
of life in New England by a "radical" Unitarian. Invaluable
for contemporary view of religious controversy.
CHANNING, EDWARD T. *Life of William Ellery.* "The Library of
American Biography"; Boston, 1837. Best source for details
concerning Channing's maternal grandfather.
CHANNING, GEORGE G. *Early Recollections of Newport, R. I.* Newport, 1868. Invaluable primary source of social conditions in
Newport during 1790's.
CHARVAT, WILLIAM. *The Origins of American Critical Thought*:
1810-1835. Philadelphia, 1936. Valuable for showing influence of Scotch realism on critics of the period.
CHILD, LYDIA M. *Letters of Lydia Maria Child,* with Introduction
by J. G. WHITTIER. Boston, 1883. Contains some important
letters concerning Channing, also parts of Channing letters
omitted by William Henry Channing in *Memoir.*

COMMAGER, HENRY STEELE. *Theodore Parker.* Boston, 1936. Excellent picture of Parker and his contemporaries. Gives Channing due credit for influencing Parker.

FERGUSON, ADAM. *An Essay on the History of Civil Society.* London, 1782. One of Channing's favorite texts and a source of many of his political ideas.

FROTHINGHAM, OCTAVIUS BROOKS. *George Ripley.* "American Men of Letters"; Boston, 1882. Rich in letters of Ripley. Shows Channing's influence on Ripley's youth and Ripley's attempts to carry out Channing's social program.

————. *Memoir of William Henry Channing.* Boston and New York, 1886. Rich in Channing letters. Especially valuable for showing Channing's influence on his nephew.

GOHDES, CLARENCE. *American Literature in Nineteenth Century England.* New York, 1944. Valuable for showing English perspective of Channing's contemporaries and successors.

HAROUTUNIAN, JOSEPH. *Piety vs. Moralism.* New York, 1932. Chapter on "The Unitarian Revolt," though somewhat flamboyant, does a good job of showing humanitarian basis of Channing's religion.

HUTCHESON, FRANCIS. *An Inquiry into the Original of our Ideas of Beauty and Virtue.* 2nd edition. London, 1726. One of the most influential books in determining Channing's ideas of benevolence.

Journals of Ralph Waldo Emerson with Annotations, ed. by EDWARD WALDO EMERSON and WALDO EMERSON FORBES. 10 vols. Boston and New York, 1909. Invaluable for personal comment on Channing.

KOCH, G. ADOLPH. *Republican Religion: The American Revolution and the Cult of Reason.* New York, 1933. Author does a good job of relating republicanism in politics to republicanism in religion.

LEE, ELIZA B. *Memoirs of Rev. Joseph Buckminster, D.D., and of His Son, Rev. Joseph Stevens Buckminster.* 2nd edition. Boston, 1851. Valuable source of intellectual background of orthodox Calvinist father and Unitarian son. Brings out difference between a literary scholar like Buckminster and a moralist like Channing.

MARTINEAU, HARRIET. "The Martyr Age of the United States," *Westminster Review,* XXXII (December, 1838), 1-59. Contains valuable firsthand reminiscences of Channing.

————. *Retrospect of Western Travel.* 2 vols. London, 1838. Laudatory account of Channing's role in the antislavery movement.

Selected Bibliography

MAY, SAMUEL JOSEPH. *Some Recollections of Our Anti-Slavery Conflict.* Boston, 1869. Invaluable primary source on anti-slavery agitation in New England and New York during Channing's late years.

MORAIS, HERBERT M. *Deism in Eighteenth Century America.* New York, 1934. Shows that deism did not disappear with Tom Paine and Elihu Palmer but reappeared from 1825 to 1835.

MORISON, SAMUEL E. *Three Centuries of Harvard, 1636-1936.* Cambridge, 1936. Best over-all picture of Harvard.

MORSE, JAMES K., *Jedidiah Morse, A Champion of New England Orthodoxy.* New York, 1939. Best treatment of orthodox opposition to liberals during the first two decades of nineteenth century.

PARKS, EDWARD A. "A Memoir of His Life and Character" in *The Works of Samuel Hopkins, D.D.* Boston, 1852. 3 vols. Standard treatment of Hopkins, who was responsible for crystallizing Channing's ideas of disinterested benevolence.

PRICE, RICHARD. *A Review of the Principal Questions and Difficulties in Morals.* 2nd edition. London, 1769. Source from which Channing secured much of his information concerning philosophic idealism.

QUINCY, JOSIAH. *Figures of the Past.* Boston, 1926. Useful for the social background of the 1820's and 1830's.

RAND. BENJAMIN. "Philosophical Instruction in Harvard University from 1636 to 1900," *Harvard Graduates' Magazine,* XXXVII (September, 1928), 29-47. Useful for showing the trend from Lockean doctrines to Scotch realism.

RUSK, RALPH. *The Life of Ralph Waldo Emerson.* New York, 1949. Thorough treatment of the transcendentalist leader although it does not emphasize interpretation.

SCHLESINGER, ARTHUR M., JR. *Orestes A. Brownson: A Pilgrim's Progress.* Boston, 1939. Best treatment of Brownson's connections with the working-class movement. Unfair to Channing and his doctrine of internal reform.

SCOTT, WILLIAM R. *Francis Hutcheson, His Life, Teaching.* Cambridge, 1900. Good general treatment of Hutcheson.

SHEPARD, ODELL. *Pedlar's Progress, The Life of Bronson Alcott.* Boston, 1937. Gives excellent picture of intellectual milieu of Boston in 1830's and 1840's. Places much emphasis upon Channing as the formative influence in Alcott's career.

THOM, JOHN H. *The Life of the Rev. Joseph Blanco White.* 3 vols. London, 1845. Definitive study of White, an ex-priest and English Unitarian who became one of Channing's most devoted correspondents.

THOMAS, ROLAND. *Richard Price, Philosopher and Apostle of Liberty*. London, 1924. Rather sketchy treatment but the best available source.

UPDIKE, WILKINS. *Memoirs of the Rhode-Island Bar*. Boston, 1842. Useful source of information concerning Channing's father.

WILLARD, SIDNEY. *Memories of Youth and Manhood*. 2 vols. Cambridge, 1855. Best contemporary source of information relating to Harvard and its graduates.

WRIGHT, CONRAD. *The Beginnings of Unitarianism in America*, Boston, 1955. Best treatment. Shows the continuity of New England liberalism.

Index

Index